50 *Do's* & *Don'ts*
for successful business networking

Rob B. Tol

Rob Tol is an entrepreneur and networker par excellence. Through running his consulting business, TOL Marketing & Communication, he has more than fifteen years' experience working on strategy, positioning and profiling in business and government markets.

Rob has worked at ABB for over ten years and spent almost twenty years with the Siemens Group. He has worked in several roles within trade, industry, cultural and ICT-initiatives. His knowledge and experience about networking is all compiled in this one book that can be read back to front and front to back. He hopes to show the benefit of networking and is giving you the tools to get to work. According to Rob, there are things you have to do and things you have to unlearn. So do and don't do certain things!

Rob was voted networker of the year in the Netherlands. He founded the Networking Academy in 2009 and gives presentations, workshops, master classes, and training sessions focused on successful business networking.

Co-reader: Judith Hentra, Book Helpline - Design: Sander Tol, TOL Design
Production: MultiCopy Capelle a/d IJssel

NetworkAcademy

PO Box 8649
3009 AP Rotterdam
Tel. +31 6 30274216
info@NetworkAcademy.nl
www.NetworkAcademy.nl

nl.linkedin.com/in/robtol

Netwerkacademie

@robtol

Netwerkacademie

ISBN 978-90-812233-4-8 Do's & Don'ts for Successful Business Networking 11/01/2016 - 500 pcs.

Foreword

These days, there's no denying that we live in a society that is networked both online and offline. Not everyone likes this but you can learn to network in a way that is more fun and more targeted.

What you also want to achieve is the following:
- No time wasted on inefficient networks;
- No excessive acquisition and research costs;
- To approach potential customers effectively;
- Tap into new business relationships;
- Have others recommend your services.

Ask a hundred people what their most important do's and don'ts are in networking and you will get just as many answers. This book provides an overview of what you should or should not do to be successful in business networking. Sometimes they are just clichés (tiles truth) and while most speak for themselves, the important question is whether you practise them.

You don't have to practise all of them to be successful.

Rob B. Tol
Networker & Entrepreneur

"Research has demonstrated
a direct link between
social capital and the quality
and meaning of life.

Good networks
increase our happiness,
our health and
extend our lifespan.

Networks enhance our
personal life and also contribute
to the improvement of the world."

Wayne Baker

What is networking?

The basis of a good network is trust. The strength of a networker is primarily to give attention. The goal is to share knowledge, information, and contacts. What matters is that you know what you are trying to achieve, how you develop your network, and how you use, extend and maintain it.

Networking is primarily about establishing and maintaining personal contacts that can be of further help to you in business. Networking is often giving and sometimes receiving help from others. So do take note of what you can do for someone else.

Networking is the most efficient, least costly, and the most fun way to achieve your goals.

There's an old saying that it's not what you know but who you know, and this is often confirmed by the business world. Personal relationships may be more important than knowledge itself and yet it is not true that they are the key to success. Think of all the old school businessmen who went bankrupt during the financial crisis of recent years. They were part of the established order and yet were still isolated from the rest. It is all about the right contacts and not just the right relationships. That is the challenge for modern networkers.

In our current networked society, it is striking that despite the enhanced opportunities to make contacts through Twitter, LinkedIn, Facebook and video conferencing, it is fairly easy to feel isolated.
Therefore, we have to make a personal effort to stay in touch.

Open your mind and explore the world. Make use of all available media. Don't forget to stay in touch with your family and friends. Keep in contact with people on your path. They also have good ideas and can help you to establish other good contacts. Moreover, they generally ensure that you keep both feet firmly on the ground.

Giving and granting means giving first

Granting is the new giving

Be happy with what you achieved, but don't be satisfied

Paying attention is art, getting attention is smart

Help and you will be helped

Networking is people's business

Help starts with good listening

The bird is known by his note, the man by his words

To get respect, you must give it

Try first to understand, then to be understood

Communication is the lubricating oil of business life

Serious interest brings serious connections

Giving compliments is nice, receiving them is even nicer

Be yourself, everybody else is already taken

Intuition tells you what to do and what not

Networking is also looking ahead

Networking is maintaining good relationships at all times

He who wants to network finds the time, he who does not finds an excuse

Out of sight, out of mind

It's yours for the asking

50 Do's
For Successful Business Networking

If you don't know where to go ... any way is ok

As you are, you are good enough

Not meaning what you say becomes not knowing what you say

Friendship is an investment in time and energy

Build a bridge and things come within reach

Networking is like breathing: don't stop

An honest man is as good as his word

Honesty is the best policy

Treat your network as you want to be treated

He who does good will meet good

Nothing is as catching as enthusiasm

Laughter is the shortest distance between two people

It's not who you know, it's who knows you

Giving is living

Forgotten to prepare? Prepare to be forgotten!

Respect gatekeepers: they can't say "yes" but they can say "no"

Social capital is like a solid, slowly growing investment

Who sows will harvest

You get what you give

Know who you want to meet

Success is as dependent on our network as on ourselves

Well begun is half the job done, persisting is the other half

It's better to be interested than interesting

Networking is all about seeing and be seen

You are as old as your network

Knowledge was power, relations are powerful

Keep in touch with the press

It's better to conform than to shock

True friends are hard to find, difficult to leave and impossible to forget

Come straight to the point

The 50 Do's of networking

Be aware of what you <u>can</u> do:

Giving and granting means giving first

1. Start by giving

The verb "giving" is in the right place in the dictionary, right before the verb "granting." A network is not only for your own benefit. The idea is that your contacts also find value in it. It is not about money. Your network operates as a constant flow of information, ideas, and contacts between you and the people around you.

Networking is mostly giving and sometimes receiving something from someone who grants it you. Determine how you can help others achieve their goals. Always ask what you can do for someone else. Granting is the new giving and an important new way of entrepreneurship. What is special is that you grant in return for something that had no economic value in the past. It's about giving others your attention and perhaps being the recipient of their attention in return. There needs to be a willingness to give in exchange for a tip or information. This can be an email address, a profile, a publication, comments, a like, or a retweet. This is not expressed in money. The intention is that there is perhaps a trade in the long term. This may be from the receiver, but it may also be from a third party. So pay the right attention and your network will work for you.

At an event hosted by Rabobank, council member John, a shareholder of an ICT-company, spoke to me. "You were responsible for the Avantage website, I hear," he said. Indeed it was me. It had been one of the first tasks from a marketing plan that I had written for them. "That also needs to happen in my club," he said. He asked for my business card and wanted to make an appointment to meet me, to see how I work and find out what my vision is. He also revealed that he himself, as an 'informal investor', was developing his own website. I helped him selflessly with tips and beautiful pictures of Rotterdam. I started giving. After talking with the CEO of his ICT-company I found some work there. It provided me with a well-paid interim project for a year.

Granting is the new giving

50 Do's for Successful Business Networking

2. Networking is mutual

We live in a networked society, both online and offline. Networking is not another word for "you give and I take." It is not "I give and then want something with the same-value-and-even-more back as soon as possible." Networking is reciprocal. It is a dialogue between people. It's a process for seeing opportunities, for pioneering, taking action, making appointments, etc. In short, it is about action that leads to reaction.

Networking is a process of establishing and maintaining contacts that help you further in your job, your career, and your personal life. But that is only one side of the coin. Your network is not just for you, it should work to the mutual benefit of you and others. The intention is for others to improve and gain as well. Granting favours is the new giving and a major new form of doing business. Help people in your network with information, new contacts and give someone just the tip which makes him happy. This is helping each other.

I met Rogier through the local business club. I told him I was not happy with the photographer I always used for documentaries. He offered his services as a photographer free of charge asking only for credit as a form of promotion in return. That's what we did and everyone was amazed at his abilities.

Any future work, we decided, would receive compensation. I occasionally work with photographers and arranged for him to work with one of my customers. He did the job very well and is now someone I regularly work with. They show me what they can do and I get them work. This also works the other way around. It provides a more flexible way of working that is more responsive to the needs and desires of the market.

Be happy
with what
you achieved,
but don't
be satisfied

3. Maintain a good personal standing

Be honest and be good at your job. Make sure you know what you are talking about and what is happening in your industry and with your target audience. Build your brand's reputation up step by step. This has to do with your personal branding. You yourself are your own brand and can thus successfully put yourself on the market and obtain the desired information or orders. Increasingly, people seek to do business with the person with whom they have had a pleasant working relationship before. It is all about developing your own talents with your competence and personal power.

Personal branding requires that you are aware of how you communicate and how you are perceived by others. You will be associated with your unique value, where you stand on issues, and what you are aiming for needs to be apparent. What is your style, what are your preferences and how do you communicate these? What are your core values in life? What are your talents? How do you channel your added value? Ask yourself how you want to be known, but stay true to yourself.

Gerbert is the founder of Virtek, a full service 3D design studio. I know him because I used to work with his wife. Gerbert produced a 3D instructional video of the salvage of the Russian nuclear submarine Kursk. The salvage division of Mammoet Shipping and Smit International has used the video for its own learning purposes. Gerbert wanted more of that kind of work and asked me during a breakfast of entrepreneurs how he could get in touch with the community and the port authorities. I told Gerbert: "I'll introduce you to the Mayor of Rotterdam who is the host of the event." Dazed, he followed me. I made a short introduction and a proud Gerbert did the rest. Since then, his business has grown to about twenty-five employees. Gerbert has become a famous producer in the maritime industry.

Paying attention is art, getting attention is smart

4. Content, processes and relationships

When people talk to each other it is about more than just the content. We speak in a certain way with each other and offer and receive words as part of an unwritten exchange. After a question we expect an answer, and after a joke at least a smile. It is a process of exchange. Of course, our feelings, consciously and unconsciously, play a large role in this.

To reach a goal, we discuss substantive issues. When people communicate with each other, time always plays a role. The topics of conversation come up in a certain order on the agenda. That is the process. The interaction is the way in which people communicate with each other, that is to say, how they react to each other. In a group, the different dynamics emerge. Who reacts to whom? Do the group members listen to each other? Do they give feedback to what is being said? How do the group members interact and how is the relationship between them? Pay attention to the content, the process, and the relationship.

I am the founder, and was the chairman, of THEMATER. We organised theme nights at the Isala Theater. The local heroes from the town Capelle aan den IJssel, who have spoken here, also get together twice a year. They are a sort of advisory board and give their support and feedback. Each month, the board of directors comes together. The location and agenda are sent out in advance. They share the tasks and for three nights a year, they welcome an average of three hundred visitors. There is annual planning and a theme each night, so we can invite good speakers and entertainment in plenty of time. We do this by mobilising our network as there is not enough budget for anything else. We always want good quality and continuity. Close attention is paid to content. In the process we also have fun. We have created a different function for the theatre: a meeting place for networking and building relationships.

Help
and you will
be helped

5. Offer to help

Helping someone with the sole purpose of benefitting in the future is not networking but bartering. With bartering, the mutual benefit only happens once. If you follow the principle of "quid pro quo", the feeling of reciprocity is not as strong. Your help may even be refused. If you help out of a genuine interest in your relationship with members of your network, if you give with no intention of getting something back, then you always create a healthy form of reciprocity. You don't know in what form, you don't know when, you don't even know which way it will come to you, but there is always something in return.

Helping people has another great consequence: because you gave your help without even expecting anything in return, you are pleasantly surprised by what you receive! If this is also given from genuine interest, reciprocity arises. You definitely want to give something back to those who have helped you so you're always on the lookout for ways to help as well.

Provide tips and help others selflessly. Treat people like you want to be treated. Help means empathising with others. It starts with listening and getting to know someone. My main question to others is, "How can I help you?" Ask but be open: "I want to help, but want some more information first." Help, but realise it should not be like work, costing you money or time. Sometimes you have to say no. Helping is also being clear: "I cannot help you, but I can give you advice." Hopefully you'll get a message later or a thank you if it was helpful. If not, that's ok. You can always ask: "Did I help you on your way then?"

Networking
is
people's
business

6. Be socially competent

People are social creatures and we all use social skills to communicate with each other. We have many ways of communicating our messages, thoughts, and feelings to each other. This involves both verbal and non-verbal communication. By developing your social skills, people are more interested in you because you are interested in them.

Most people know that you don't get ahead in life without personal relationships. Focusing on relationships will help to obtain a job, get promoted, and make new friends. But you have to communicate! Do you need help or a favour? Then don't assume that you won't find it from someone else. If you don't ask, the answer is 'no', no one will help you, but if you do ask, 'yes' is an option. If it is important for you, and the other person is capable then just ask. Most organisations are looking for people with the ability to work well in a team. So make sure you are able to connect with people at different levels, to build and maintain relationships.

At network meetings, I usually start talking to a stranger about a general topic. It might be regarding the location, the host, or a news item. The talk is a lot more relaxed speaking about a topic you are both interested in. In the end, we usually exchange business cards. Within a week what I might do, for example, is send an email about something we talked about, accompanied by a tip. This contact might not provide exactly what you are looking for, but it could be the start of a good relationship. You can bet that the person remembers you from that point on.

*Help
starts with
good
listening*

7. Listen closely

Some people can talk your ears off without ever realising that they are only having a conversation with themselves; the other person has long since stopped listening. A conversation is a two-way method of communication. The fastest way to build trust and build a relationship with someone is by listening attentively. This saves time and stress and in turn you get valuable information and realise how valuable someone can be for you. Genuine and sincere interest in someone starts with honest and open listening. This gets the attention because people don't experience it very often.

Listening is a gift you give to people in your network. Listen carefully to gather information and respond deliberately. Also listen to what is not being said. You can listen on four levels. Just listening dutifully is hearing. Selective listening is hearing what you want to hear. When listening attentively you are completely focused on the other. Empathic listening is active listening in order to understand someone. That's what it's all about!

I know from my own experience that listening is not my strongest point. To keep my attention on the conversation I do my best to visualise the information. What I have learned is not to react impulsively. Instead I try to give myself time to think before I speak. Don't think you need to only listen half-heartedly and just to go along with what someone is saying. Be curious and attempt to be as candid as when you were young. Encourage people and don't interrupt them when they're talking. Show that you are interested, ask open questions and be quiet for a moment. See what opportunities you can create with what you have heard. How can I use this information? What have I learned? What can I do with it?

The bird is
known
by his note,
the man
by his words

8. Let others express themselves

You've probably seen this before: a group of people standing around at an event. One is talking more than the others. If a timid person finally tries to tell his story, the rest interrupt him because they cannot wait to talk about their own experiences. Often such a story gets bogged down. If someone does tell their story then often others just talk over it. This can be very annoying and even rude.

In a conversation, try to keep what you want to say to yourself and listen to others. Don't be impatient. Bite your tongue if you have to, or count to ten. Are you bored by how tedious the others are, then respond at the right moment. A discussion can get well under way by sharing experiences, but let the person talking finish first. Don't finish their sentences for them or guess at what they want to say even though you might be enthusiastic and want to talk about your own experience as soon as possible. Let people express themselves and be silent for a certain amount of time. You will be amazed at how others come up with relevant information.

My flaw used to be that I did not let people speak up nor did I compliment them. Sometimes I would even say what I thought they wanted to say. It was an extremely annoying and rude habit. I experience this myself when others do it to me. My partner points this out to me regularly and I have now trained myself to keep my mind on the speaker and not react impulsively. I suspect that I have lost contacts and even lost business with that behaviour in the past. That is what I very much admire in introverted people who let others quietly express themselves, and journalists or doctors who have learned to listen professionally. You can even get training to control your listening techniques.

To get respect, you must give it

50 Do's for Successful Business Networking

9. Be respectful

Networking requires an active and respectful treatment of people in your social circle. Everyone wants to be treated respectfully, and to get respect you have to give it. This is the main rule to respect when networking. Appreciate people for their qualities, their performance, or their skills. Those don't only have to be people who have a high position on the social ladder.

Try to respect the views of others, even when you don't share them. Appreciate people's own values. Respectful networking is a way of networking where the other person feels they are truly heard and understood. This involves a process of asking questions, ascertaining the needs and desires of people and making trust central. Don't ask suggestive questions and certainly not things that can be embarrassing. Part of respectful treatment is being aware of your own values, relative to those of the other. Are you aware of how you engage people?

If you are respectful towards people, I know from my experience that in just three simple steps you can reach every individual businessman or businesswoman. This certainly applies to politicians. Suppose I want to approach our current prime minister. The former one lived in my area, which made it relatively easy. I know a councillor in my town and via him, I organised for a member of parliament to be a speaker at an evening about city branding. I also spoke a few times with the mayor of Rotterdam. My partner plays bridge with the former secretary of the prime minister. Through her I could, if I wanted to, approach him! Worldwide it is six degrees of separation. It's a small world...

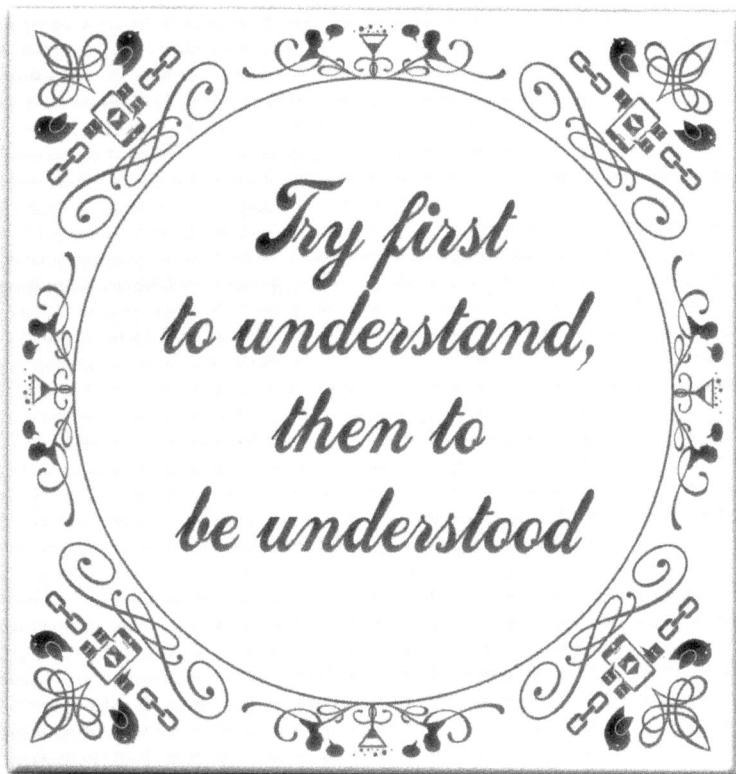

Try first
to understand,
then to
be understood

10. Understand what people mean

Communication between people does not always go smoothly. You don't understand what the other person means or the other person does not understand you. Some people talk at cross purposes. In communication, both the transmitter and the receiver are responsible for a good transfer of information. People who communicate clearly are able to clearly convey their message, to feel, and understand what the other means. If you can't listen to what others are saying then you can't understand what they really mean. Without understanding what the other person means it is very difficult to add anything meaningful to a conversation. Often you find that people control a discussion and express their own views. Try first to understand and only then to be understood.

By reflecting back in my own words what another has said, I make sure I have understood him. Don't make this summary too long: a word or a sentence is often enough. It is about the core of the message. "If I understand you correctly, you mean ..." Being good at asking follow-up questions is a kind of art to be learned. By following up on what someone is talking about, you can get to the core: what really motivates someone, what does he really want, and why is it so important to him. Often there is a lot behind the why. I often ask open questions in a conversation or interview. These are phrases that begin with who, what, where, when, why and how. My conversational partner then feels better understood and I invite him to tell his own story.

Communication
is the
lubricating oil
of (business)life

11. Communicate

There is so much information everywhere that people want to keep their world small. The flow of information has now been reversed by the internet and social media. The sender no longer determines what people see; it's now up to the recipient. He decides whether your information is relevant, and emotions play a big role in this decision. The way you communicate should suit you. Let people know what you are doing. Use various communication tools and invent clever combinations. If you see or hear something interesting, remember to whom it can be of service.

A relationship is based on good contact. If you want to be successful in the long term, you need to keep communicating to maintain the ties of your relationships. Business is about constantly binding and making connections, even beyond the boundaries of your business and increasingly across borders. Networking is an integral part of that process. Without good communication, you are often unable to convey your thoughts and ideas in business networking.

From experience I know that the leaders of a company often work months in advance to develop their strategy. After much deliberation it gets written down and communicated to the middle management. The members of the management team should work to keep this strategy alive. It is extremely important to involve the employees early on so they can take on the chosen strategy. If they are involved in a timely fashion, then they can give their support and will be generally willing to do their part. It must therefore be clearly communicated so that employees know what the leaders mean. Communication is the lubricant that makes everything happen smoothly.

Serious
interest
brings
serious
connections

12. Show real interest

It seems as if genuine interest in other people is now a strange characteristic that has started to fade away. With sincere interest you bind people. Pretending you are interested in those in your network is counterproductive. Be interested in someone's story. Showing genuine interest is also a kind of basic attitude. People love to talk about themselves. Knowing that, you don't have to do much to make people feel comfortable. Let them talk and listen carefully and sincerely, without searching for a business link, a chance to provide input or a lead. The remarkable thing is that if you show genuine interest in others, others often show interest in you or are willing to listen to you if you share the things you are going through. People like people who like them or have the same interests. As you are someone who has shown interest in them, they want to right the imbalance (which they feel unconsciously) and show interest in the other.

Showing genuine interest is difficult for salesmen, because at the end of the day they think that something must be sold. Which salesman gets the best sales? The one who really listens to his customers. Isn't it wonderful when someone is listening to you attentively? The man or woman who is really interested in the people they work with or do business with is the one of whom everyone says "What a nice guy". That is what they mean when they say, "He has that x-factor." So, it's the one who shows genuine interest.

Giving
compliments
is nice,
receiving them
is even nicer

13. Give compliments

After a sincere compliment, relationships prove considerably more amenable than before. Every professional or entrepreneur has quiet times in any given month. During such moments share an additional compliment. Browse through your links-, customer- and prospect database or glance through your business cards from recent networking events. Send a sincere compliment to at least five contacts.

Take a look at the website of a contact to see if there is any good news.

Also read blogs and financial sections of newspapers to see if there is any news about companies you know. Send an email, sms or app to your contact person with a sincere compliment. Sometimes you get an immediate response, but don't take it for granted. If you contact them after a while to make an appointment or come across him, the response to your compliment will always be positive. There is also nothing wrong with giving someone a compliment face-to-face. It is a small effort but it gives great pleasure!

I read on the website of someone with whom I'd like to do business, that they won a large contract. I congratulate them and pay them a compliment. They like the attention. I now have a nice contact. When I read an article or interview with a colleague or client, I cut it out and send it or the online link with my compliments. Sometimes I send the whole magazine to a potentially interested contact. Or I scan certain information and send it together with a nice letter with compliments. I also send things like this by mail sometimes, for information, to multiple stakeholders.

Be yourself,
everybody else
is already
taken

14. Be yourself

Be yourself. Don't act or behave extremely different. Don't imitate anyone.
You are unique. Pay attention, however, how others behave or misbehave at a
networking event and learn from them. After all, no one is perfect. But how
can you be yourself in a world that is constantly changing and demands so much
of you?
Our years in school teach us how behave when we are angry. We need to think
about what we say and if you can't say anything nice then it's best not to say
anything at all. This is what drives you further away from yourself. Society does
not always appreciate your passion when you say what you think but it is then,
when you act upon your feelings, that you are most powerful. If you truly follow
your passion, you stay enthusiastic. You stay pure, sincere and trustworthy.
Practise shows that it is not easy to be yourself. You need to have the guts for it.
Make sure you accept your limitations. Turn your weaknesses into strengths.
Be yourself, which is hard enough!

*If you want to be authentic, it is important to reduce learned behaviour. This is a
process, such as when you want to unlearn being silent just to keep the peace. So it is
important to consider in such situations what you actually think and feel. Answer
without thinking about what others think of you. It is your answer; your truth. The
only one who should agree with that is you. If you just regurgitate what comes out of
an entrepreneur's mouth, it reduces your value to them. I notice that they at times
need to take a fresh look at a case, at the arguments and objections. Individuality is
much better in the long term.*

Intuition
tells you
what to do
and
what not

15. Listen to your intuition

It is hard to listen to your intuition, but it is important to break through limiting patterns. Often you will notice after an event that you actually felt what your intuition was trying to say. If you want to develop your intuition, then it is necessary to understand the thoughts that block and hinder. People usually don't like change. They are frightened about the risks they think they see. A nice side effect of researching your limiting patterns is the realisation that they affect you in more than the one area of your life that you have in mind. If, for example, it is your anxiety that is limiting you, then once you work on this theme you will see the benefits in all areas of your life and not just in relation to networking. Therefore, listening often leads your intuition to further growth and development.

In networking, intuition plays a bigger role than you think. Don't mistake networking for opportunities in sales and business, but instead see it as an opportunity to meet interesting people. These people also have interesting contacts. Often you are in a conversation with someone and you find out that you have shared relationships, or even know the same people. Also common interests, for example, music or a holiday, can be a clue. I notice that a connection with someone often follows.

Networking is also looking ahead

16. Think long term

Networking is like a private relationship; all contacts are formed step by step. Through the short-term attraction, conquer and surprise, to long-term connection on to deepening and extending the relationship. The main value of a network is not that you can arrange all sorts of things at short notice. Its value is more important in the long run. A good network is something you cherish and that you build with care year after year.

Your network provides early signals about the market and what will happen. If you keep that in mind, doing business is a matter of scoring an open goal. You know what happens in the league and in the field. If you network regularly, you stand in the centre of life and you are socially active. You pick up new ideas. Through networking you rarely score new projects or orders in the short term. Networking is about investing in a relationship for the long term.

I was looking for an active entrepreneur as speaker for a local event. I ended up with a general manager of an ICT-company. When we met for the briefing, he told me that his company needed a marketing communication approach. The sales director had already had extensive talks with several agencies and the general manager put me on the shortlist. I was able to present my approach. After a few weeks the news came that they had not chosen me. Of course I was disappointed, but still remained in touch. After half a year I was called again. The chosen company had not performed well and it turned out I had a better approach. I have been working with them for ten years. During that time I didn't mind putting in the extra time to bring them positive publicity.

Networking
is maintaining
good
relationships
at all times

17. Maintain your network

You have built your network and expanded it and then comes the hardest part: maintaining it. People need to regularly hear or see something from you. The longer you keep quiet, the harder it is to make contact again. Networking requires maintenance, regular doses and intense targeting. Whenever an opportunity for contact comes up then use it or create a moment to contact someone yourself. It is often enough to show interest in others and you can do this by telephone, email or through social media. Send an occasional email with news and visit fairs and business meetings where your network is. It allows you to maintain your network and even expand again. Be sure to have your news on your website and send regular communications to your network about this. An old-fashioned letter or a 'With compliments' card now and then provides the feeling of paying attention, especially about something that is interesting to the recipient.

I often invite one or more contacts I know to an event already taking place or I create one myself. Those I invite can bring with them someone they want to introduce or their partner. This is how I maintain my network and also how I expand it. As the host, I make sure my contacts have a memorable day, but I also don't forget to enjoy myself. In business, you have to deal with people who like attention. Nowadays it is also possible to stay in touch by mail, sms, app or tweet. A business associate of mine calls these 'sparks'. Don't be an opportunistic networker who only seeks contact with people when you're doing well. Your friendly contacts may be disappointed if you do not contact them when you are leading the way. This is especially true when they hear it through the grapevine. Maintain your network, therefore, at all times.

He who
wants to network
finds the time,
he who does not
finds an excuse

18. Network even when busy

Network not only when it suits you, or when your order book is looking bare, because at those times you want things to happen quickly and others notice this immediately. What follows is stress and unnecessary irritation.

Make time at the beginning or the end of a day to maintain your network. Try to make it to an appointment on time. It is especially at busy times when you must put in the extra effort for networking. By the time you desperately need projects or turnover it is too late.

Clients and customers should not notice any pressure, just because you are currently like a puppet on a string and at the mercy of your reputation and price. The dysfunctional relationship between supply and demand in times of recession and particularly the reluctance of clients makes sure of this.

That is the tough reality. Of course, an entrepreneur should always network. Be especially careful with your network. By regularly listening carefully to customers, you create more revenue and in the best case scenario you also get new customers. So ensure that customers continue to be loyal, and get from you the attention they deserve.

At networking events I often hear the same trashy catchphrases from tough entrepreneurs: "My business is booming," or "Busy, busy, busy." Other entrepreneurs who don't have the same pressure say: "Shall we see what we can do for each other?" or they actually cry out, "I need work." What works better is a good relationship. At times when you find yourself working day and night, you want only one thing: for the job to be finished and for you to get some rest. Once that happens you'll find yourself enjoying it for only a few days before doubt quickly appears. "There will surely come a time when there is some work again?" you start to ask and so you go networking with eagerness. The person who you approach senses that you need work. That is why I deliberately network when I am busy too.

Out of sight,
out of mind

50 Do's for Successful Business Networking

19. Keep in touch

Also make contact when you don't need anything from anyone. People notice fast if you only contact them to ask for things. In families there is always that family member, that uncle, who after months of no contact, calls to ask for help or a favour and usually as soon as possible. The conversation often starts with: "Are you doing anything next week?" You can feel the request for a favour coming up. This is also the case in business.

We are all busy in our own way so make sure you regularly keep in touch. Maintaining good contact with someone means not only sending a card at times of celebration but also contact them just so they hear something from you.

The longer you avoid this, the harder it is to make contact again. Whenever an opportunity for contact comes up, use that moment so that the connection stays friendly. It is often enough to show interest in one another. I remember a campaign that went as follows: "Send a card. Little effort but great fun!"

You can do this either by telephone, email or through social media. Businessmen also like attention.

I developed the 'Network Roundabout' for regular contacts. I create three occasions in the spring and three in the fall with about hundred clients, so that the friendly relationship stays friendly. For other contacts, several times a year are sufficient. Make sure you have news and stay positive in the media. Give presentations, workshops or teach at a school. I quickly get to know those who just get in touch if they need something. After all, we are all busy, I understand that, but let others regularly hear from you.

It's yours
for the asking

50 Do's for Successful Business Networking

20. Ask questions

It is remarkable how many people struggle with asking for what they want. What would happen if you asked for something? It may be that you don't get exactly what you really want, but don't be discouraged. Chances increase when you make the art of asking your own.

Is your goal clear? Do you have a serious question that does not cost money or take up too much time from others? Then ask the question! Make a list of the people who can help you to achieve what you need and regularly remind yourself of it. People often don't dare to ask for help or information because they are afraid of being rejected or being seen as annoying. They struggle to show off their vulnerable side. In reality, people feel generally flattered and respected and are happy to help. With a lengthy, unclear or confusing question, the chances are you won't get the information you need, so be clear about what you are asking and don't hesitate. Also ask how you can help others with their goal. Often a nice connection is established which is then up to you to maintain.

When I visit a meeting or an event for the first time, I often use the following opening question with a visitor: "How do you know the organiser?" Then, if I want them to remember me, after our introductions I ask a question that they won't be expecting. For example: "What do you like most about your job?" I sometimes invent an original open question which shows that I have a particular expertise. If you cannot invent a question on the spot, do it in preparation for the next meeting you'll be attending. Remember, it is always possible to ask something!

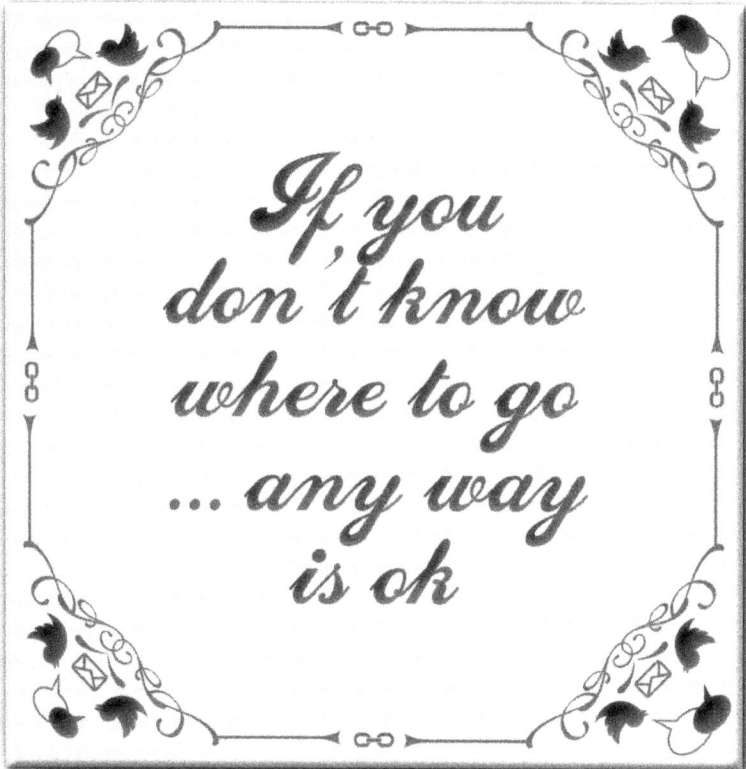

If, you
don't know
where to go
... any way
is ok

50 Do's for Successful Business Networking

21. Know what you want

Create a short and powerful business- or strategy plan, so that the objectives and actions with which you want to achieve your goal are clear. It is not about the plan itself but about creating the plan. It makes you think: What am I doing? What exactly is my goal? What am I good at? What is my passion? In short, what are my ambitions? Create a network plan of a few pages (see no. 50 do's page 109). Build relationships by reading and finding out in advance about the person you will be talking to, his circumstances, needs and any problems. Also think ahead. Prepare for a meeting and ask for a list of participants. Check the website and LinkedIn. Provide an elevator pitch. Don't do it automatically, but always say something that will make others smile. People ask questions sooner, remember you better and will remind you at crucial times of events you may not know about. Or they will recommend you when people in their network ask something such as: "Do you know the right person for that vacancy?" or "Do you know a good specialist who I can ask for a quotation?"

Be good at your job and know exactly what you want and what your target audience wants. Arouse interest through your knowledge and experience. Make sure you get remembered in the marketplace: "That is the man who made some interesting remarks." "That is the woman I've read about." "That's the man I've heard many good things about." Become and remain well known for your target audience. Try at least to get published in your local magazine or website by sending out a press release. The local media are also important. I make sure people in my network know what I am looking for and what I want to achieve. In short, what my goals are as an entrepreneur.

As you are,
you are
good enough

22. Present yourself

Leave an unforgettable impression. If something happens in your field, people will remember you, or better still, they will seek you out. In the business world, non-verbal communication is just as important as anything else. As much as eighty percent of business decisions made are based on other factors, such as a connection with someone. This has everything to do with body language. It means that you need to be curious and exude confidence. Things such as eye contact, a handshake, an open body posture, smiling and nodding are all examples of good body language. Your handshake is often the first opportunity you have to make a positive impression on someone. Don't give someone's hand a squeeze or shake with a limp hand, especially not to women if you are a man. All these things contribute to doing business with pleasure and to effective networking. The idea that effective networking is only reserved for extroverted people is a blatant misunderstanding. Whether introverted or extroverted, both can benefit by networking.

I always know how to start a conversation anywhere and about anything. I love to be in the spotlight and be surrounded by people. These stimuli give me energy and make me move around easily in meetings. I often have trouble however with good and focused listening. Introverted networkers often struggle to introduce themselves. They first think carefully before they open their mouths and aren't much affected by ice breakers. As they observe and feel things, they get a better understanding of others. They are often good listeners and only focus on one item at a time. They are the ideal complementary conversationalist.

*Not meaning
what you say
becomes
not knowing
what you say*

23. Be confident

You are the expert in your field with all the necessary knowledge and experience. Remember, don't be shy and talk yourself out of the picture. You stand for something, and you know what you can do and for whom. Be confident about yourself and show this to people. To come across convincingly you need more than just the content you use. Content is important, but how you present it will determine whether it is powerful and convincing. When in conversation your body language determines your impact. It is about your attitude and the tone of your voice. What you say exactly appears of less importance.

Be aware that everything you do will be heard, seen and experienced. It is your performance that makes you effective or not and this is especially true when you give presentations. Try to communicate the same message verbally and non-verbally. You are then in alignment with yourself. What you think, feel and do is in balance. Don't constantly question yourself or wonder how people look at you and think about you because you then get off balance. That will then be apparent to your audience. Always be sure of yourself.

I once gave a presentation for a group of marine engineers. We were waiting for the general manager. I was allowed to start and what I had to say was well-received. After half an hour he arrived and the atmosphere immediately became cooler.
He slouched indifferently in his chair. I interrupted my presentation and asked him politely if he was interested in what I was saying. Once I engaged him he sat up attentively and even asked a question. On the way back home I wondered whether I did the right thing. My partner advised me to write to him about my vision: "If he doesn't appreciate that, then he is no client for you." I wrote the letter with the thought in mind that "I won't really post it." I sent it anyway and within a week I received a letter with an apology. I got paid for all the hours I invoiced them and they sympathised with and respected my position. So stay confident about yourself.

Friendship
is an investment
in time
and energy

24. Empathise with others

Empathy is the degree in which you take care of the feelings and needs of others. If you have a good radar about how an organisation works, formally and informally, then you already practice this.

Empathy is not just about feelings and emotions. You may also be sensitive to the objectives, interests or desires of other people. In short, pay attention to the feelings of others in the way you behave. Keep them valued and put yourself in their position. Show that you recognise the feelings and needs of others. Be aware of the impact of your own actions on them. When you have an appointment with someone, prepare for it. Google their name and look on social media. What are their hobbies, sports, education, membership and family composition? How is their business doing? What are the problems in the industry? Can you help them with solutions so they can say: "You know what I mean!"

Specific people, or people who have specific skills or knowledge, can be accessed through networks via other people. Professionals are connected with each other on LinkedIn. Users are motivated to keep their profile (CV) up-to-date since they are contacted based on this information. If you have an interest or a contact in common, you can use this to break the ice. Keep track of the professional activities of people you know. I find people with specific skills, knowledge and experience offline in my network, but also online. LinkedIn is a useful tool for this.

Build a bridge
and things come
within reach

25. Connect people

According to the dictionary, the following means building bridges: "Connect two groups so that there is mutual understanding." A bridge connects two worlds that were previously separated and symbolises the exchange of ideas and experiences. You notice what is happening in the market and think, "Who could I make happy with this information?" and without immediately thinking of yourself.

Connect people and step back. Pass on new information and knowledge that you already have. Also do this with other subjects and industries in which you are not involved. That is what networking is. The better you do this, the more you are able to get the most from your network. Ask proactively if you can introduce someone to another. Introduce them to each other and give a short and positive introduction. Also be a matchmaker at a distance. If you have a friend who is an architect and has been looking for work and you find a developer who is looking for an architect, you can refer him. Act as an intermediary in your network.

At one of the business events in my neighbourhood, I got into a conversation with Glen. He was the branch manager of an accounting firm and gave me a brief and clear understanding of its work. He doesn't care only about cents and percents. I told him, that when I started my business, I had a large accounting firm working for me. I missed the added value for my business and switched to George at a small local accounting firm. He did not aspire to work with big businesses. I like to build bridges and so I connected George with Glen. At the next business event Glen told me that there had been an order for him through George. The bridge worked quickly and is now working the other way too.

Networking
is like
breathing:
don't stop

26. Have broad interests

You are as old as your network so keep rejuvenating and modernising. The environment, the market, and the customer are constantly changing. To survive, your network must be varied. Changing contacts and cultures strengthens your network. Read literature and management books. Watch opinion programs. Go to a different trade show and make contact with people outside your industry. Visit museums, exhibitions, concerts and theatres. Watch how colleagues tackle their business and learn from them. Also listen to young people and get inspired. Be consciously open to the upcoming generation and new media. Purposefully participate in social media and blogs. Successful networking is largely dependent on the initiative that you dare to undertake. Get out there and be curious about new developments. Diversity also plays an important role because it makes you stronger if your network consists of different types of people with various origins and professions. Seek out and also make contact with people in politics, sports, education, creative industries, and retailers.

Do you know how your colleagues and competitors operate in the market? Certain other industries and developments may come your way. Discover them. Think of innovations and disrupted technology. New markets will be created with values and networks to the detriment of current markets. I go to presentations and meetings, not only about my profession but also from neighbouring areas. I Google and learn about interesting information and innovations. In the social media area especially, interesting things happen. You don't have to apply the information directly but be curious. You will be amazed and sometimes astounded. In short: be broadly interested, not only for yourself but also for your customers and associates.

*An honest man
is as good
as his word*

27. Keep your word

When networking, fulfilling your promises is crucial. Promises, promises. The promise is a kind of guarantee. It determines the quality and continuity of the relationship. Fulfil your agreements. If you can't do so then let it be known in time. Someone who does not fulfil his commitments, or doesn't even try, is unreliable. This quickly gets known via the online media that are available. An expectation is already surpassed when you send something at the correct speed of delivery, when you call back, or provide the right personal attention and expertise. When you promise to send someone documentation, some mail or to find out certain information for them or to call them back, then make sure you actually do. These days it is surprising enough when you do what you promise. If you do more, people are really surprised. Under-promise and over-deliver. This is of vital importance to a relationship with someone to keep it friendly. So keep regular contact and fulfil promises, otherwise this will get known in your network.

"If you do not fulfil all your agreements now, then you might not do so in the future either," a prospect thinks. However, if you are responsive, alert and effective, you are a few steps ahead of all the others who have been lax in keeping their agreements. Recently, I was contacted by my current provider when they wanted to offer me a smartphone in order for me to renew the subscription. On the face of it, I was interested. We agreed that they would send me an email with details. On principle I never do business by phone. I never received that email. Too bad for them, because I was actually looking for a new smartphone! Now I have one of their competitor's, who sticks to their agreements.

Honesty
is the
best policy

28. Be honest

If you are honest, you are often most at ease. This gives you a natural and reliable appearance. Don't exaggerate and never lie. A prolonged network relationship is based on mutual trust. Honesty is indeed the best policy. As an entrepreneur you would like to make an indelible impression on potential customers and associates not only during an elevator pitch, sales conversation or networking event, but also on paper. And, of course, online: on your website, blog, Twitter, Instagram, Facebook and definitely on LinkedIn.

The advantage of a talk or presentation is that you can look each other straight in the eye. Is there static on the line? When together, you can add nuance or clarify a point so that you are again directly aligned. Direct interaction is lacking in print or digital media so choose consciously to project an honest message. Avoid expletives and container concepts. If you want to be seen as honest then show your cards and have a consistent message on paper, online, in talks and during presentations.

As a starting entrepreneur I didn't dare to say 'no' because I really wanted to generate some revenue. This, alongside a healthy amount of bluffing, helped me land a complicated job. I soon realised that I had taken on too much and after a week of struggling, I decided to leave the job. By that point, however, I had made a bad impression: I had a frustrated client and a dissatisfied customer. I came across convincingly, but was too eager. You need to be honest: dare to say 'no' to tasks for which you don't have the capacity, knowledge, experience or affinity. Only say 'yes' to jobs when it is a resounding 'yes'.

Treat your
network
as you want
to be treated

50 Do's for Successful Business Networking

29. Thank people

Remember what people have done for you, show your gratitude and try to do something in return in any form you can. Thanking people takes a small amount of effort. If you get a tip or an invitation, let them know that you appreciate it. It's a thoughtful thing to do. People find this pleasant and you get in contact. They'll remember it next time.

A great way to strengthen your network is a thank you email, sms, app, note or a personal thank you. Even though you may not be able to use that tip, thank them for it. It is always well-meant. Someone has thought of you. If you can do something with it, let them know what eventually happened. Maybe you can make someone else happy with it. Tell that to the tipster. People like it. Thank a tipster through whom you have had a great event or whose advice led to a contact or an order. Put in a special thanks when it ended up bringing you business.

My former colleagues hold an annual reunion. It's nice but it's also an opportunity to network. Everyone's gone their own way. Anecdotes are shared, there is drinking and laughing together and business cards are exchanged. At one of these, I bumped into Pim. We had always worked well together at Siemens. He was in contact with an ICT-company. He said, "You've started a communications bureau? You ought to contact the owner of this company who is looking for a man like you! I'll introduce you to him." That is a word-of-mouth recommendation and the best thing that can happen! It really generated work. I thanked Pim very much and he can always count on my help.

no. 30
do's

He who does good will meet good

50 Do's for Successful Business Networking

30. Pass on an invitation

Always say thank you for each invitation and let others know in good time if you will attend. If you decide to go, then show up, otherwise let them know in time if you cannot. From my experience, I know that there are about fifteen per cent 'no shows'. A new phenomenon is that people don't sign up and still come under the guise, "You know I always come when you invite me!" This typically happens at recurring events. This isn't a good thing for the organisers who have to deal with catering, but also for the visitors who have expectations about who they will meet there.

If you already know when you receive an invitation that you cannot attend, then let them know! Do you know someone else who would enjoy the event, if it's not a personal invitation? Then ask the person inviting you if a colleague who shares the same interests can come instead. That is often mutually agreeable. Sometimes there is an invitation that is strictly personal and it is obvious that the intention is for you to go rather than someone else.

Every year I receive a pair of tickets for a special free night at the Rotterdam zoo. However, I already have a subscription to this zoo. If you receive multiple tickets to an event, think "Who can I make happy by helping them go or taking them with me?" Your contact's partner often plays an important role in the background. Try, if you are introduced to him or her, to make a connection and find out what he or she likes. Do they like horses? I always receive free tickets to the Concourse Hippique. They can have my tickets. This also applies for their son at the cycling races or for a boxing gala.

Nothing
is as
catching as
enthusiasm

31. Find common interests

Networking is based on finding things in common. It does not work if you go on a meeting to an important person and talk about how wonderful you are. What you get is a sympathetic smile and him looking for a less intrusive partner. Instead, begin with small talk about a general topic. During the conversation you will find out, without having to ask, where his interests lie. Talking about a topic you are both interested in will be more relaxed. Ask for a business card afterwards. A few days later, you can send an email in which you refer to the conversation. You can also pass on some news about a topic you discussed. This starts off the foundation for a good relationship and a build up of trust. You bet he'll remember you!

Shared interests can range from being fans of the same music to liking the same holiday destination. Through Google, LinkedIn, Facebook and Instagram you find people with the same interests as you. People that you have never met before are now no more than a click away from you.

I remember well some advice a relation of mine gave me when visiting a director of a construction company. I provided some successful training focused on business networking for his colleagues. The conversation with him was a bit stiff and we babbled on until he started, just offhand, talking about motorcycling. This was David's passion, which unfortunately, I didn't know about beforehand. It is also my hobby. His eyes began to glisten and we got into an animated conversation about our motorcycles. The contact was immediately much better.

*Laughter
is the shortest
distance
between
two people*

32. Have fun

Especially when doing business, humour puts things in perspective.
Don't take yourself too seriously. Business decisions are made primarily on the basis of non-commercial grounds; on the basis of a connection made.
You create a relaxing atmosphere and this contributes positively to a better contact. You really don't have to love everyone, but if you are going to a meeting then try to go with a sense of fun.
Some people unfortunately see networking as a technology or a task they have to perform. A necessary evil. You hear sometimes: "I have to show my face" or "My boss told me to go there." As a result, they miss the opportunity to really connect with people and build a relationship with them. So don't go to an event reluctantly because that works counterproductively. This doesn't only apply to corporate network relationships but also to personal ones.

I am not good at telling big jokes to make people laugh so I don't attempt it. A quip suits me better. I try to do it in context. In presentations I enhance awareness with the use of funny videos, illustrations, and quotes. Music also plays an important role.
I pay attention to my appearance, my entrance and my presentation. I dot my serious message with a wink and a nod every now and then. By having real fun you increase the chance of a connection with others. I know from experience that you are more effective at networking if you enjoy it.

It's not
who you know,
it's who
knows you

50 Do's for Successful Business Networking

33. Network on several levels

Ask yourself how much a contact's position can be helpful to you achieving your goal. For decisions to be made, several people are involved and each has their own interests and responsibility. These are decision makers, influencers and stakeholders.

Are you in touch with the right person, in the right place, at the right time and do you also make contact with relevant colleagues? You know only one contact in a company? That is a small base. If this person leaves, the chances are that you lose the relationship with that organisation. Make contact, for example, with manager or colleague of your contact, but please note that you still need to value the current contact and don't just ignore him. Also, in a large company, make contact with other departments too. By networking you also find out how everything runs within an organisation. Who actually pulls the strings; who has real influence? Is one decision-maker strong enough? Or do opinion makers around him play a major role and should you address them in particular?

A manager of a club of communication managers where I was a member called me to say that he had an interim job in an ICT-outsourcing company. It was an internet project in the middle of the Netherlands. After the project was completed, I was asked if I wanted to do a project in their office in the north of the Netherlands. Here I met the managing director and gave a presentation at his request at a staff meeting.

I became quite well known within the organisation. After this project was completed there followed an order from their office in Rotterdam for a special direct mail campaign. I always take care to make multiple contacts at various levels in a company.

Giving
is living

50 Do's for Successful Business Networking

34. Make sure you know more

Make sure you know enough about your contacts, such as information about business deals, interests, and hobbies. I am not talking about gossip. What makes them tick? So not only their address details (name and address) but also memberships, partner, family composition and birthday. Learn something nice about your contact. What did he study? What keeps him busy? How can you help him or do him a favour?

Once you have some interesting information from your contacts, it is wise to write it straight down. At the back of the business card you have received, for example. Write down when his daughter is graduating, when his son goes to Australia, when is his first day at a new job and so on. Once you see in your calendar, CRM or Outlook that there is something important happening for your contacts you take action. You can wish them good luck, send a card, email, sms, app or just call. In short, give them attention at just the right moment.

In my network I know a person whose son is a baseball player. The World Port Tournament is organised in Rotterdam every two years. My son was a baseball player too and I like this great sport! If I cannot go to a tournament or if I have more tickets than I need, I will give them to a contact. When I buy two tickets to a jazz festival for a business friend, I know I'm doing him and his wife a great favour.

They can go together or, if it fits our schedule, I'll go with my partner and join them. Takes little effort but gives big fun.

Forgotten
to prepare?
Prepare to be
forgotten!

35. Prepare for visits

Prepare a visit to a prospective contact very well. Scroll through their website, look on LinkedIn, and Google their name. Ask yourself what business you are going to discuss with them. Get there on time. Try to have a little chat with the receptionist or secretary and even bring some trivial gift for her. After the introductory meeting niceties, start on the important part: the coordination of goals and expectations. Close with a specific action or appointment and fulfil this as soon as possible!

Check the entry list if you intend to visit an event. Think about where you want to sit and next to whom and about the people you want to speak at lunch or dinner if there is no seating arrangement. Ask yourself: do I need to be there? What exactly is it all about and who else will be there? You don't have to show up to everything! Are there people you would like to meet who have something note-worthy to say? Or are you just going for fun? There is nothing wrong with that, but do not have high networking expectations!

Let me step back in time to when I was a beginner networker in the nineties. I am at The Hague at a networking place I have never been to before. I walk into the building and pick up a badge. Meanwhile, I'm thinking: "Are there any interesting people here?" I do not see anybody I know. I order a drink. Other people come in. I wait until someone starts a conversation with me, but no one comes my way. The other people talk. They all know each other. I'm thinking: "How will I ever make contact with them?" From behind a folder I have found, I look at them surreptitiously. I look at my phone and visit the toilet. I come back but it doesn't get any better and half an hour later I leave disappointed. A lost evening. I should have prepared and requested the list of participants.

Respect gatekeepers: they can't say "yes" but they can say "no"

50 Do's for Successful Business Networking

36. Keep secretaries as friends

Secretaries, and also assistants and receptionists, know what is going on in their offices. Make contact with them too and stay friendly with them. They are the spider in the web and everything passes through them. Make sure they are your ally. They know the diaries, customs and habits of the organisation, its departments and employees. They know the unwritten rules. What can you do for them? Pay them attention, a compliment and sometimes bring them a little present. You literally and figuratively can't get past them. If you want an appointment by phone with a major businessman, you are often confronted with them. They will do everything to not connect you with their manager.

They want to know everything before deciding whether he has time for you. In addition, a secretary will try to connect you with an employee who could 'better' help you, or they will try to help you themselves. If it is not to her liking, she will raise all sorts of obstructions: "Can you send the documentation first? We will call you if we are interested." It is important to treat secretaries with respect and to appreciate them.

If you are having some difficulty getting past a secretary, then praise her: "As a personal assistant of Mr. X, you know what is happening within the organisation! Do you know what his schedule is like?" Or "Perhaps you can help me. I would like to make an appointment with Mr. X, but do not know exactly how I can go about doing this in your organisation." Mention what you are calling about. If a question like "What exactly is it about?" comes up you will have your short elevator pitch ready. Don't try to bluff her with terminology, but be clear about the solutions you have. She will hopefully connect you with him at some point and point out that: "This is a nice man who has called several times. He would like to speak with you about ABC. Here he is ..."

Social capital
is like a solid,
slowly growing
investment

37. Be active in a club

There are several possible ways to add businessmen to your network. LinkedIn is a handy digital tool. If you want to meet people in person then search for business events. Becoming a member of an association or club has a lot of advantages. You get to know new people and you have the opportunity to help them with the chance that they want to help you too. You build relationships of which some might bring long term contracts.

Become an active member of a workgroup or administration but move on after a few years for another opportunity, which is refreshing. A network is for those who know that a good network is the foundation for entrepreneurship. Experience, sharing knowledge and doing business in a regional network is the value of a membership. The network needs to keep its members fascinated through meetings on interesting topics and bind its members through informal events. The meetings come first but doing business is always permitted. Remember, you get out what you put in.

Before founding my agency, I became a member of a regional communications association and after that of the local business association and the World Trade Center Club. I visited the evening events faithfully and soon volunteered as project leader for the second-generation website of the communications association. As a result, I was asked to help to introduce an ICT-platform. The outcome of that was that I became a contractor for the City of Rotterdam for one and then for two days a week in the Department of Finances. In my first year, I won the Best Performance Growing Entrepreneur in Rotterdam North. This gave me a lot of free publicity. I was asked to be a member of the Members' Council of the Rabobank. I also organised Rabo theme nights. As a volunteer I worked in the area where I live and work. My network grew and grew. So make sure you are active in a club; it brings you a lot!

Who sows
will harvest

50 Do's for Successful Business Networking

38. Sow thoughtfully

To get results from networking, you first need to sow before you can harvest. This means that you invest in new contacts and maintain them. Be open about yourself and pay attention to others. Try to listen carefully to the person you are talking to. After you've listened, talk about yourself, your work and about what your passions are. This is contagious and gets others to do the same. During the first meeting you might not see immediate ways of collaborating. Just make sure your name stays on the other person's mind.

Sowing does not mean planting as many seeds as possible, but the right ones at the right time and in the right place. When the time comes, you harvest. Forcing it does not help. On the contrary! Try and have a pleasant conversation with some people. This can produce more than a pile of business cards. More than anything, have patience. You are like a farmer who sows. He does not expect the plants to sprout the following week. Sow actively within a network. After some time you will notice that you can start harvesting. This might be in the form of a tip, a conversation, a collaboration or even a contract.

I myself have a metaphor: the grapes in my garden. I once put a small plant in the ground in the sun. I gave it water and fertilizer then cut and pulled away the weeds. The rest came naturally. You can't do more than that. You cannot give that plant more water or fertilizer. You can however weed, provide some support and protect it from the wind. You put your energy into it. You enjoy it and you then enjoy the harvest. The foliage keeps the bright sunshine away so you can sit in the shade. I pick the first grapes in September when they are ripe and blue. When I give them to my family and see their enjoyment, my own enjoyment triples! We also make delicious grape juice from them. It is the same with building, maintaining and exploring your network.

You get
what
you give

50 Do's for Successful Business Networking

39. Network proactively

To wait and see is not the point of networking. You need to be active both online and offline. Networking is a matter of discovery. Approaching someone new may feel awkward but remains the most important lesson. Consider that the other person probably also finds it interesting getting to know new people. But if you just go somewhere where you've known everybody for a long time then you might as well stay home.

Someone who does not network in today's networking society is probably unsuitable as an entrepreneur. Networks can deliver a strengthened bond with a contact. It increases involvement in your activities and creates support. It gives you support, understanding, inspiration, new perspectives and ideas. In the long term, you can actually generate work with networking. Also, it can help you to achieve the desired function or job you are applying for. You will learn through informal processes. It is in the corridors where you learn what is really going on. Active networking promotes your well-being and gives you joy because you meet different people and gain information.

I have an agency that I built especially through networking. My network was my capital when I started. I kept people around me who were not on my payroll. Thus I had some breathing space no matter how the market was doing. Before I founded my company, after a career as an employee, I was an active member of a regional communication association. I am closely involved in the organisation of regional initiatives. I play sport three times a week and at the sport club I am also active in a team of sporting friends. I am a volunteer in the district where I live and work. As a result I have become visible to many people. I have written books about my activities. With other writers I founded a writers' collective. So I stay in the picture.

Know who
you want
to meet

50 Do's for Successful Business Networking

40. Make use of your network

Targeted networking is not just about having friends. It is all about the knowledge they can provide. In business markets you should ask yourself to what extent a contact, through their function, can be helpful in you achieving your goal. Organisations are made up of several people and each has their own interests and responsibility.

Make sure you get in touch with the right person, at the right time and also make contact with relevant colleagues. Your network can provide better answers to your questions once you know your own business goals and what you want to achieve. These questions, around which your network can mobilise, can provide some insight into your network's goals and come up through self-examination in the long run. Who can help you to achieve your goal? Through social networking it is easy to make contacts and to engage your contacts. You see what engages your target group by asking questions and actively responding to questions or sending them interesting content. This helps you remain in the picture. Turn to your network if you know who you want to meet.

To get help or to get a useful answer or a referral, you have to ask the right questions. For example: "Would you help me with...?" I know now that, especially in a small country like the Netherlands, you are only three degrees away from reaching the business person whom you want to contact. On LinkedIn, this is easy and accessible. LinkedIn also shows the second- and third-degree networks and the paths towards them. It finds the right people and the interesting connections for you. This is of great value and brings you closer to your target audience. More and more organisations are deploying business pages on Facebook and entering into dialogues with their contacts. With social media, you simply turn to your network.

Success is
as dependent
on our network
as on ourselves

41. Organise an event

Successful networking depends very much on the initiative that you dare to take. People don't come to you by themselves. Create an event or meeting by yourself. It doesn't have to cost much. See the costs as an investment in your network. Mention that your guests can bring a guest of their own. You are offering your customers a networking opportunity. In this way you maintain your network. Make sure as host that the guests have an unforgettable time. Send a press release and invite journalists and editors to witness the event. Just as long as you have news, of course.

You can even invite a few contacts together to an event: to a trade show, conference or contest, combined with a joint business lunch. Organise an event or organise something around an event, but do it well with a good plan and comprehensive planning. Your guests must not want for anything. Give them something appropriate afterwards and make sure that photos are available. Most people like to be in the picture. Make sure your contacts speak positively about it in their network and try to make a tradition of it.

When I first started the communications agency in 1999, I used to rent a boat on the river Meuse for my network. We would sail to the Information Centre in the south of Rotterdam. I introduced my situation and tell them that it's where I started working for myself after a long period at Siemens. Back on board, we would sail further with a band and some drinks. I'd give all my guests a copy of my first book and a fountain pen to get their opinions and reaction. At our five-year anniversary, I rented the Euromast tower. Here I handed out my second book. My best customers were the first to get it.

On my tenth anniversary we celebrated in the information centre of the steamship Rotterdam and we sailed with a passenger tender round the ship. The visitors also got a ticket for a tour with the amphibious bus in the river and through Rotterdam.

Well begun
is half
the job done,
persisting
is the
other half

42. Be consciously present at events

Try to arrive early at a conference or a workshop. Ask for the participants' list, if you haven't already received it in advance. There is often a copy at the check in and it is often available. The advantage of arriving early is that you can quietly take your place in a strategic position in the room so you can have an overview of the entire playing field. The speaker is usually very early and would like to know what the audience is like. Find out in advance whether they've published something and Google their background. Ask something early on and ask for their business card. It may sometimes happen that they'll mention you in their presentation. Afterwards you can be more relaxed when you speak with him.
If you want to speak to someone who will otherwise be difficult to get a hold of, make sure you are in his vicinity just before the official presentation, breakfast or lunch starts. Try to walk near and sit down next to him. Greet acquaintances and go to someone who you see standing alone. They also usually want to expand their network and feel relieved when someone begins a conversation with them. If you decide to leave, thank the host, say goodbye and then go.

Be careful with what attitude you enter an event. Go with the following mindset: "This seems to me to be a great opportunity!" Are you alone? Ask for the host or organiser. Perhaps they can introduce you to someone. Observe the comings and goings. Make eye contact with someone and start a conversation with an open question such as "What brings you here?" I always try to find something in common. Move on and talk to other people every now and then. Does an event not really suit you? Accept this and go to meetings where you do feel at ease. You will then be much more accessible and open to new contacts.

It's better
to be
interested
than
interesting

50 Do's for Successful Business Networking

43. Have your elevator pitch ready

Many people can't manage to introduce themselves clearly in one minute. That is unfortunate because the first impression is the most important.

This is especially true for entrepreneurs and job applicants because if the attention slackens, they might miss out on a customer, an assignment or a job. So prepare your elevator pitch. Make it a small piece that briefly but powerfully introduces you and makes others curious about you. It is important that you think about how you want others to remember you.

Occasionally someone will show more than just polite interest after your elevator pitch. That might be the sign for making a contact so say something like, "I notice that you are interested." Don't answer elaborately, but ask a few more questions and arrange for a time to meet. You have scored a 'hot lead', as it is called in the sales jargon. A short elevator pitch is fine but after that it comes down to asking, listening and communicating. If you talk for too long it irritates people. A short introduction is good. A long introduction is deadly.

An elevator will take one minute to arrive at its destination at the top floor of a building. During that time you have to introduce yourself personally to another person in the same elevator who asked you and is waiting to find out what work you do. This is why we call it the 'elevator pitch'. This should be a starting point for a conversation. It is short, powerful, and crisp. The best thing is if there is a question. Ask the other person what they do and then ask for their business card. So, who are you, what do you do and where? What can you do for someone and why? At the end give an example of a client or project you are particularly proud of!

Networking
is all about
seeing and
be seen

44. Attention to business cards

Networking is about building relationships, not meeting a lot of people and collecting business cards from them. Also, not about throwing around business cards. The purpose of a business card is a symbol in itself. This usually means that the person who gives the card would like a continuation of the contact or hopes that you will now recommend him to someone else. It's likely that some people will even give out two cards. First, ask for a card and receive it respectfully. Look at it carefully and ask about something on it or pay it a compliment if you like it. Most of the time, the other person will also ask for your card. If not, ask at the end of the conversation whether you might give them your card.

If you are in a meeting and on the other side of the table are some new people, then lay out the cards you've received in the order which the people are sitting next to each other. If you forget someone's name you simply cheat and check. Are you the president or host of a first meeting, then ask upon entering for people's business cards and copy them beforehand on a piece of paper then hand out the cards. In this way you prevent a situation of just handing out cards for the sake of it. Just make sure you have enough business cards with you. You could even keep a supply in your suitcase and in the glove compartment of your car.

Collecting business cards, joining no conversation and then bombarding these people with useless emails is senseless and time-consuming. I note on every card I receive the date, meeting place and any appointment that gets made so that I don't have to wonder, "Who was that and what did we arrange?" Unfortunately, there is usually no picture on the cards. I recommend you add a received business card into your database within a couple of days. The business card is often, after the first impression of someone, the second impression of his organisation. Make sure yours radiates what you stand for. So pay sufficient attention to business cards.

You are
as old
as your
network

50 Do's for Successful Business Networking

45. Expand your network

Expanding your network often comes naturally when you are proactive. In business and in your private life you will meet new people and thus create new opportunities. You can approach people in order to focus on your goals, for example, by calling for an appointment. While many people find this difficult, it is mainly a matter of doing. You will then naturally find that networking is often enjoyable. Sometimes you also give advice to others, because you have more knowledge in a particular field than they do. You probably find yourself doing that with pleasure and commitment. This is also the case for the person you approach to network with. Don't force yourself to devise a new networking act. Don't overdo it or lay it on too thick, because then networking becomes contrived. A simple and quick, but unusual, way to expand your network is to ask existing customers if they know of any new customers. Research indicates that seventy percent of new customers come from some form of networking. If our network is twice as large, it is four times as useful for members.

Before I started my business, I banked with a different bank. They did not have an interest in my new situation. At Rabobank, a cooperative bank without shareholders, they wanted me and I was even asked to their Members' Council. This is a representation of members and an advisory board to the board of directors. I was very active there for twelve years. They asked me at the time to do something for the local community. Together with the director of our city's theatre, who was also in the members' council, I developed the concept THEMATER (Topics at a Theatre) with a few other members. By the end of 2013 we had existed for ten years. We organised about thirty evenings with an average of almost three hundred visitors per evening. My network keeps expanding more and more.

Knowledge was power, relations are powerful

50 Do's for Successful Business Networking

46. Organise your network

I recommend you: map your network and organise it regularly in a database. Start off with the question "Who knows me anyway?" This in itself is an exercise in awareness because it is important to know who knows you. If you know someone, how well do you know that person?

Create the list in Outlook or in your relationship management (CRM) categories in your contacts. Otherwise sort the business cards you've received into different categories and into several fields. For example, the categories might be your work, your sport or your alumni. Networkers maintain a secure smartphone with all addresses, phone numbers, email addresses and data. In this way they can help people with certain contacts via search facilities even when on the move. They synchronise with their notebook and vice versa. If you know people through others and you have a code for this then you can find them easily. Research shows that an active entrepreneur knows about 500 people. That's wonderful because each of them knows on average 500 people in turn. So you can, without much effort, reach 250,000 people!

Every spring and fall I make a printout of all my contacts from Outlook, to walk through, clean up and update during a quiet period. You can use the information in your database to bring people from your network in contact with others. To help them further with things that you think they could use or to ask for advice. Structure your network as a mind map and make sure you begin to enjoy this. It can cause a chain reaction. You get an idea of contacting someone, this gives you a good feeling, you react, call or mail and often something positive happens. LinkedIn offers this by Maps.

Keep in touch
with the press

50 Do's for Successful Business Networking

47. Network with the press

Coverage from independent journalists and editors has a higher value and more authority for readers. Realise that sometimes you lose the grip on your message. You can ask to see the text before publication, but usually you may only correct substantive errors in the content. By keeping journalists, ones who write in the industry and region where you work, updated with good content you will create a mutual understanding and you can count on sympathetic coverage. So don't only call or email them if you want them to get something done for you, for example, getting your press release or an interview published. Network with them too, so when you need them, the contact has not gone cold.

When people from the press ask you something, help them as soon as possible or let them know that you will find out from the appropriate person and call them or mail them the information. Do what you promised because you will need them again. With poor contacts the reverse of what you want can happen. So keep in regular contact and help journalists and editors as soon as possible if they ask for information or artwork. In short, try to make contact before you want to get something done in the press.

I try to maintain a personal relationship with journalists and editors in the ICT-sector, where I worked a lot. It is not easy to get their attention and you can't get that just with a press release. They don't mind if you give them a call after you send the press release, but they hate it if you keep pressuring them to get something in the press! After all, they receive dozens of press releases a day. There are often changes in newsrooms and they are not as interested in your commercial news. Call a journalist not only when you have something new but invite him to have a chat. Obviously you have to have news so give him some news first. To generate publicity for clients of mine in relevant magazines or sites, I network with them. So, try to network with the press too, not only for yourself but also for your branch, your customers and network.

It's better
to conform
than to
shock

48. Be a chameleon

A chameleon literally adapts to its new surroundings. It does so in order not to attract too much attention. It is the nature of this animal. It also has highly developed eyes with which it can view its surroundings out of the corner of its eyes.

A good networker also adapts himself and takes the playing field into account. He is well aware of its uniqueness, but nevertheless takes into account various situations. He also puts himself in other people's shoes and has respect for local customs and habits. If he deviates from this, he does it not to shock or offend the people around him but on purpose. Everything is done with respect. He always prepares himself well and dresses appropriately for meetings. He will consciously adjust his clothing to the expected conditions and match the dress code if an invitation specifies it. Yet if you do look a little different, people will better remember you. It is the detail that makes someone different.

Years ago I was invited to a magazine event at a polo match. I have no real interest in horses, although I was, through Siemens, involved in the sponsorship of the horse event CHIO Rotterdam. On arrival at the polo match, everything was well prepared. My car was parked amongst big jeeps and I sat down between ladies of the upper-class. It was an elitist event and nice to experience for once. There was champagne and caviar.
I was well prepared with my choice of outfit. I had found out that the dress code was Business Casual Smart so I had chosen neat khaki pants with a shirt and a jacket. The habit to kick over the clumps all together during the breaks surprised me a little bit because of my new suede shoes with leather soles. However, it was a great networking opportunity for meeting others out on the open field. Back in the tribune I could smell the stable air. That made sense because it was coming from under my shoe...

True friends
are hard to find,
difficult to leave
and impossible
to forget

50 Do's for Successful Business Networking

49. Use social media systematically

Our society has become much more individualistic. People are less likely to be active members of traditional organisations such as political parties, associations or clubs than they used to be. The decrease in these opportunities to meet up means that you should make a greater effort to make contact yourself. Opportunities for contact offered via the internet and social media are a useful tool. They can help entrepreneurs find, increase and keep their audience. Organisations in business markets are learning how customer relationships can be improved with social media.

You need to associate social media with your business goal: what do you want to achieve and how can social media deliver added value in achieving this objective? Using social media in combination with other communication and personal contacts is very convenient. There are new companies with no webpage but who immediately start a corporate business page on Facebook. Try to convert online contacts into offline ones, but don't force it. End a message with a question now and then. This helps bring interaction from the communications.

According to researcher, Richard Dunbar, one hundred is the theoretical limit of how many people you can have a relationship with. Try to think of your one hundred and fifty business contacts. Dunbar claims that most people have five true friends and no more! I use Facebook, LinkedIn, YouTube and Twitter deliberately and selectively. On Twitter, for example, once a week I post a networking tip. My followers like that and not the non-informative stuff they often get. Also, for a whole year I tweeted about a celebration or sport event that was happening that day. My followers would join in with their own communication. The things I can post won't dry up. I now have these 100 do's and don'ts to post!

Come straight to the point

50. Create a network plan

Know what you want to achieve with networking and prepare yourself well.
'Smart networking' is done with a plan in which you formulate your goals in
advance. Create a network plan and do it SMART as part of your business,
policy, or development plan. It is not the plan itself that is important, but to
think about what you want to achieve: Who would you like to meet to help you
get closer to your goal? Who would introduce you? Where actually is your target
audience regularly?

The network targets I want to work for are SMART:

Specific
What contacts do you want at any level and who/what can you help with those?

Measurable
How do you know if you've reached your goal? Can you measure it?

Acceptable
Is the goal acceptable to all involved: participants, colleagues, and the organisation?
What disadvantages are possibly connected to the goal and how can you work around this?

Realistic
Is it feasible in terms of time, budget, in the current situation, and with your level
of competence?

Timed
By when should your goal be achieved?

The do's are often things that you normally already do, but could be better for your network. Try it in conjunction with the don'ts, which you'd better avoid.

Be aware of what you definitely can do:

1. Start by giving
2. Networking is mutual
3. Maintain a good personal standing
4. Pay attention to content, process and relationship
5. Offer to help

6. Be socially competent
7. Listen closely
8. Understand what people mean
9. Be respectful
10. Maintain your network

"Who you know is just as important
as what you know.

If you built the right network,
you get the help you need
when you need it.

Networking increases
the quality of life
and your ability to be successful
especially in the information
and communications era in which
we now live and work."

Wayne Baker

You don't know what you want? You'll never get it!

If at first you don't succeed, try, try again

Give without remembering... receive without forgetting

A business friend in need is a friend indeed

Be sincere and you will do well

Grass doesn't grow faster by pulling it

Dig your well before you get thirsty

Instead of thinking, "What can I get?" think, "What can I give?"

No news... good news? Quite the opposite!

You can choose your friends but not your family

Give money, you lose it, give attention, you receive something

A rich network gives you more than a fortune does

Birds of a feather flock together

It clicks or... it does not

There are contacts you should grant your competitor

Reputation comes on foot and leaves on horseback

Well done is better than well said

Nothing influences more than recommendations

The bigger the ego, the harder the fall

What's past is past

50 Don'ts
For Successful Business Networking

Give, but don't give away your work

Thou shall not stereotype

Put your cards on the table

The world becomes smaller, your world becomes bigger

If all things are equal, people prefer to buy from friends

He who cannot tweet will never be retweeted

What's done is done

Small gifts maintain the friendship

Look before you leap

Who are you? Who knows you?

Like knows like

Don't search high and low

If you drink, you become another being... with more thirst

Don't hurry someone

Actions speak louder than words

You can't judge a book by its cover

The more people you know, the more you know

We're in this together

Fine feathers make fine birds

Hear no evil, see no evil and speak no evil

I don't have an office, I am an office

Asking questions makes you wiser

Don't look over someone's shoulder

My name is nobody

It's not what you say, it's what people hear

Knowing you is loving you

Support the one you see in the mirror

Hollow phrases sound the loudest

No second chance for a good first impression

Your face speaks volumes

The 50 Don'ts of networking

Be aware of what you should <u>not</u> do:

You don't know
what you want?
You'll never
get it!

50 Don'ts for Successful Business Networking

1. Networking as the goal itself

Many entrepreneurs take part in networking meetings for the wrong reasons and then don't succeed in participating in something meaningful. They see networking as a goal in itself. Networking should contribute to your goal in the long term and not be the goal.

Network to see if together you can become wiser. It is a game you have to learn to play honestly together and not one used to score quickly in business. You should have a goal in mind. "What do I lack, what do my contacts lack, how and where can I find a platform and how can I use this to cater to my needs or the needs of my contacts?" Someone who really is networking is doing it not only for himself, but also for the people in his network. You will thus be rewarded threefold: firstly, by your networking contact, the person with whom you connect, and finally by yourself. See networking not as a goal but as a method of doing business nicely.

Suppose you have access to a number of seats in a theatre for people you know. For well-known artists you have no problem getting these seats filled. It's the same with the corporate boxes at football clubs. When Feyenoord plays against Ajax, the corporate box cannot be big enough. But when playing against De Graafschap you invite acquaintances just to fill as many seats as possible. Was that the point? Targeted use of the chairs would be more meaningful. The theatre, or sports team, undoubtedly has a list with other companies with available seats. Talk about these companies with your most important network members and ask them in which ones they are most interested. The seats then provide more value and benefit for everyone and throughout the year!

If at first
you don't
succeed, try,
try again

50 Don'ts for Successful Business Networking

2. Passive networking

You cannot network passively. Waiting until someone somewhere contacts or invites you will not get you where you want to be, especially not if you want to be known to your target group. You don't have to be an ADHD networker, hyperactive and active everywhere. Many people find it difficult to approach a stranger and yet it is that simple: that person will usually want to make contact and will often be relieved when he is approached at a networking event. Showing genuine interest in people is how you get a conversation going.

There are three components to determining the success of how you transmit information and influence: your words count for just seven per cent; your voice thirty-eight per cent and your facial expressions and gestures for more than half of the way you communicate. So be relaxed and speak in a friendly tone.

If you want to speak then start the conversation talking about general things and move on quickly to topics that interest the other person or things they enjoy. In short, let the other person feel understood and part of your circle.

As an entrepreneur or professional, you need to let yourself be regularly heard and be seen. Don't overdo it; do it in a way that suits you. I am active in various fields, often take the initiative, make eye contact, introduce myself and ask what the other person does, and I show interest by asking questions. I try to actively listen and remember clues or common interests. Then I ask for a business card and give mine.

If the other person asks me what I do, I start my elevator pitch. I show respect, end the conversation on a positive note and in time, make an appointment, stick to it, and stay in contact. That is how it (net)works!

no. 3
don'ts

Give without
remembering...
receive without
forgetting

3. Networking as a trick

Don't see networking as a marketing trick and don't do it in a contrived fashion. It is no abracadabra or magic formula. Networking is a way of life and not something you do occasionally. It is a lifestyle that fits your own personality. Be yourself, take the basic rules to heart and practise them.
It involves attention, authenticity, commitment and listening skills. Do what you promised and get noticed in a positive way.
Try to have a little fun. You don't have to go anywhere and hide who you are. Be yourself and let my do's work through you. Networking is about paying attention. That is the right attitude and not some trick you've learned. That just doesn't work. Notice in your conversations with others whether there's a chance to help them. First focus on relationships and then on business.

I get many questions along the lines of "How do you network?" It is not a trick, a technique, or a science. It is more an intention, a philosophy, a real belief that networking is the simplest and best way for me to achieve my goal. I give a lot and people pass on information to me. In the long run it brings me, as an entrepreneur, a great deal. Also, I often get the question: "Can you learn to network?" I have heard that ten per cent of people are born networkers and ten per cent just can't do it. The remaining eighty per cent can improve or learn how to do it.

A business friend
in need is a
friend indeed

50 Don'ts for Successful Business Networking

4. Expecting help

Don't expect someone to spontaneously help you, even if you've helped those people in the past. If you don't expect much then you are rarely disappointed. If, with your commitment, you manage to help someone get out of trouble, then, of course, they are grateful right then. You become energised by this response. Everyone loves compliments and gratitude, but in today's hectic times, people quickly get back to their daily business.

People forget quickly, often unconsciously, how they were helped. Remember the help you have received from people and forget the help you have given. Make sure to ask networking contacts and friends for information and assistance. If people cannot help you, they could at least refer you to someone who can. Remember that people basically like to help others, but they need to know with what they can help.

When I became networker of the year, several people around me said that I had to do something with this title. But help to take action doesn't just appear out of thin air. I asked for a meeting with Bert, one of my business friends, and we had a chat with my partner too. He gave me some feedback on the plan I had already produced. He had some good ideas and comments. As we said goodbye, his heartfelt advice was: "It's up to you to do it, Rob!" I quickly founded the NetworkAcademy, a website was built, I published my first book and created a plan for a masterclass about networking. Not long after this I introduced Bert to Henry, who got him to teach a module in account management.

Be sincere
and you will
do well

50 Don'ts for Successful Business Networking

5. Feign interest

Don't pretend to have a great interest in the other person as this immediately becomes apparent. The impression you often make is that you want something from them or that you are selling yourself and your product or service. That is not always a bad thing and there are people who understand this, especially if they are interested in buying something from you. It is learned behaviour, techniques and skills in the interaction between people. Sometimes it is manipulation.

In our consumer world, people are encouraged to use a variety of techniques so that others will like them. Or they are encouraged to feign interest to get something done. This is not networking. People need to be in contact with others. They need each other in order to learn from the other and move forward together. You show genuine interest by working from your heart. People unerringly sense if interest is sincere. You are not interested in someone at a meeting? That is possible as there isn't always a spark. Thank them for the friendly chat and keep it short, be polite and say you also want to speak to other people. There is nothing wrong with that if it is honest and sincere.

"How are you?" How often have I asked someone how he or she is doing but have I really listened to their response? It has become a central part of starting conversations but with no content. If you are genuinely interested, and ask sincerely, then beautiful things happen. If you are interested in what people say then others appreciate it. You get a whole different conversation. So ask the person sincerely or don't ask at all. Also don't ask hastily. Make time for it so you can be more specific and follow up even when the answer is a simple, "Well." But what is going well?

Grass doesn't grow faster by pulling it

50 Don'ts for Successful Business Networking

6. Forced networking

You don't have any appointments? You have little or no work? You have just graduated and want a job? Then you have actually started networking too late. You are forcing the networking: calling, spamming, mailing and pushing. This is counterproductive. Be honest; you yourself are also not impressed by this. Make sure you network in a timely and structured way the whole year round. Networking just to network is wrong because networking is a tool and not a goal. Graduates are now finding out that they will no longer automatically get the dream job they had in mind. Due to the recent difficult economic times, many have lost their jobs and have been forced to retrain or start on their own. Usually they are on LinkedIn with statuses like "in between jobs" or "looking for new opportunities." But this will not do: you should think carefully about what you want and then go for it! Networking is critical to your success, so make sure your added value is recognised and accepted.

Workers are fired in a bad economic climate and have to find another job. Some start their own business and they are then faced with a small network. Often they hadn't seen the usefulness of networking but now the situation has changed dramatically – they have to! They are forced into networking. I must admit that when I started my business, for the first three months I didn't have enough work. At times this caused me to doubt I would get any work and I was too forced on my network to find something. My network only started to work for me when I stopped forcing the matter.

Dig your well
before you
get thirsty

50 Don'ts for Successful Business Networking

7. Networking when you have to

Has your sales pipeline dried out or is your income stagnating? Then, unfortunately, you've come too late to networking. Network regularly and not when you're desperate. It's at those times that you urge people to buy something from you or your partner. You become an uninvited guest because you want something from others straightaway. This is irritating and hopeless. You can't just enjoy small talk anymore and you end up in a vicious cycle. Make sure this is not happening to you and keep networking, even when you are busy; when you are working on a temporary project; when you take a long vacation abroad or a sabbatical of a year. In a year when you're not doing any work, it is understandable if you stop networking! But you can occasionally let someone hear from you, especially with the current online media. If you don't maintain your network, you are done for when you get back in town.

I regularly maintain relationships by making appearances here and there. It's important. Even if you're an employee, it is becoming important to build your network and to maintain it. In work appraisals, this is, and in my opinion quite rightly so, a separate area for review. Do you have good intentions to network or have been ordered to do so? Or have you yourself planned to network perhaps? With an unenthusiastic appearance at an event it's hard to connect with anyone. Try to make the most of it. You're an employee rather than an entrepreneur at these events so it's not your earnings that are at stake but it could directly affect your position!

Instead of
thinking,
"What can I get?"
think,
"What can
I give?"

8. Sales tricks

In networking, the sale of a product or service can come about as the result of a prolonged contact that has been built up with respect and care. Networking is not the same as sales.

The more you are interested in helping, the more success you will have. The more you push yourself as a seller, the less success you will have. Networking involves watching, making contact, asking questions, listening, being interested, empathising and, especially, giving. So find out how you and the other person can help each other. Find points of agreement and call on links with other people in your network. Networks provides a solid basis for good business results and results in other areas of your life. Share knowledge, share information and only sell when you are sure someone is hinting that they want to buy.

An entrepreneurial spirit and professional ambition are both associated with networking. With a more or less healthy balance between work and private life, however, there is no place for two evening-filling sessions per week. I have experienced it myself. Hence the popularity of networking or business clubs that keep it simple and offer nothing more than just a platform for establishing business contacts. As long as participants don't confuse networking with sales then no one has a problem with this way of networking. In commercial networks, it all comes down to how to contact a potential customer or even better, to have an informal meeting with them.

No news...
good news?
Quite the
opposite!

9. Not staying in touch

Many families used to say on parting, "No news is good news." With networking it is just not the case though. Even though you are busy, occasionally show your face or send a message. This is easy with the current communication tools. It requires only a small effort!

No matter how busy you are and where you are, this should not be an excuse to neglect your network: for example, freelance workers who don't keep networking because they are too busy with a project at a company. No messages from you makes a bad message for your network. Imagine yourself when you don't hear anything for a while from someone in your network. It makes you wonder why, especially if you are trying to get in touch and get no response to your mail, text message, or a belated response to a voice mail.

I know self-employed people who freelance for a certain project or for a specific period. This is a period where they don't find new work. When the project finishes then they get back on the market and find it remarkable that their network does not welcome them back with open arms. In fact, they must do their utmost to show that, after a period of radio silence in their network, they are back and available once again. Sometimes I work temporarily at an organisation for one or two days a week. This way, I still keep in touch with the business world, but I also keep in touch with my network.

You can choose
your friends
but not
your family

10. Neglect your family

Your family is your first network on which you depended entirely in your youth. Cherish your family members and take care in maintaining regular contact. Nowadays, family companies are doing remarkably well. This is partly because of the close relationships of the members and also because of them consciously wanting to leave something good for their children. Unlike your friends, you don't choose your family. You can neglect a friend, a love may leave, but a family member remains family. Have you neglected your own family when you have been busy? When the work is done, you end up sadly alone. You should therefore slowly build up your family network again.

Research shows that a lot of help comes from family members. Active parents help their children. When they get old, the children take care of for their parents. Knowing what your family does can be useful and it brings fun. Conversely, it is useful that they know what you are doing. You don't have to talk about your business at social events, but you can be pleasantly surprised if they can put you in touch with your target group.

Compared to when I was a child, our society has become much more individualistic. Families are smaller and we don't automatically go to relatives' special occasions, and people live farther apart. Marriages break up and households are smaller. Spending your whole life working for the same boss is not standard anymore. Also, people don't necessarily live and work in the same area and they are less often active members of traditional organisations such as political parties, churches, unions, associations or clubs. The decline in these obvious contacts means that you need to put in more effort to make contacts. On the other hand, many self-employed people work from home, so there is more contact with their families.

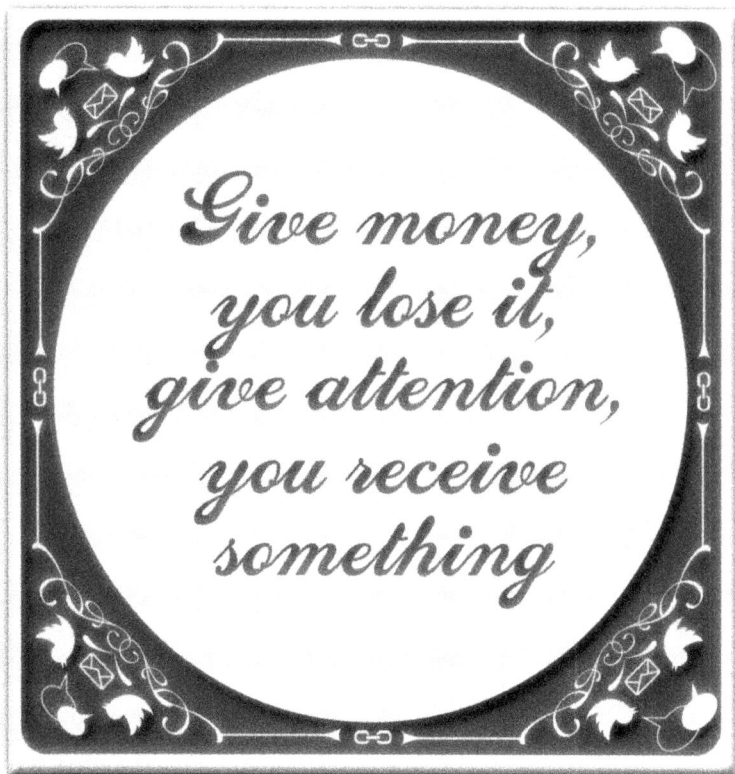

Give money,
you lose it,
give attention,
you receive
something

11. Keep a balance sheet

A well-maintained network is like social capital for business but also works for personal purposes. A network is not only for you, it is an intention that your networking contacts can also profit from. It is then not about dollars.
If you give away money you have lost it. If you give attention or knowledge you get something in return sooner or later. Your network operates as a constant flow of information, ideas, and contacts between you and the people around you. An essential part of networking is granting.
Networking does not work like a balance sheet: "I gave you something and you are now in my debt. I would prefer something back of the same value or more." A good network is a solid, slow-growing social investment for the long term. Networking is, after all, an investment for the future.

Networking enables me to simply create value, to get things done and to achieve goals. Using social capital is more about investing than asking. It's more about giving than receiving. If you have invested in social capital, you can often count on people in the long term. Social capital grows, unlike money, the more you spend it. The more people you help and serve, the better your reputation, your network and the access you get to resources.

A rich network
gives you more
than a
fortune does

12. Earn with networking

Many people see networking as a way of quickly making contacts and then seeing if they can do business with them as fast as possible. It does not work like that. You don't have to network with uninteresting people, but only networking with people to benefit from them is the other extreme. Surely it is give and grant, even though the proverb says give and take. Taking is so negative.

Remember that what somebody has given to you is more important than remembering what you have done for someone else. Through their networks, your relations, acquaintances and other people have access to much more information than you might think. Make sure you are important in the sector your contacts are involved in. They should want to do business with you. Use and don't abuse your network. When you meet someone new and your attitude is, "He has nothing to offer, I cannot earn anything," then you aren't really listening. That could be a missed opportunity.

Targeted networking focuses not only on direct but also on indirect target groups. Nowadays other stakeholders also increasingly determine your success. When do you ever really know whether you can do business with someone? You will need to get together. Someone doesn't need anything at first, has no commercial potential as a decision maker or key player? Through experience, I have found that if someone has a role as an adviser or influencer, they may also be an important contact in your network. Also end users, consultants, teachers and journalists are important contacts.

Birds of a feather
flock together

50 Don'ts for Successful Business Networking

13. Only soul mates

How often do you see, for example, people on exhibition stands talking to each other? Or during a corporate event, salesmen clustering together without regard for any of the people around them who are showing an interest? This is not the point of the event. When there is a plenary meeting or a presentation, they don't sit among the attendees. At a business lunch or dinner with clients they even sit next to each other, while the intention is for people to mingle amongst their contacts or network.

At many entrepreneurial events it would be good to just mix with officials and entrepreneurs, instead of standing around with senior officials. These people may prefer to talk to each other despite the opportunity to find out about what is happening in the business world and the market. Greet your colleagues and talk to visitors. You can then hear what is happening and entrepreneurs feel welcomed and heard.

Arthur is a regular visitor of a business club. He has been a member for ten years. Every time he attends a meeting, he is happy to see the other six members who he met when they all attended the first event. They have so much to tell each other that the evening passes before they realise it. It is always good fun. Sometimes they do business. Everything goes well. Or does it? Last time, Arthur began to wonder who the other members were. He would love to have talked to them, especially since he would love to get some new customers. When talking to the other members, however, he would feel that he had abandoned his friends. I advised him to discuss it with his friends.

It clicks
or...
it does not

50 Don'ts for Successful Business Networking

14. No click: it's a pity

A connection with someone feels like kinship, finding a kind of soulmate.
Don't be disappointed if you don't make that connection or feel that click with
someone you meet. Perhaps you'll learn something from them which will help
you do a favour for someone else. Don't force the connection.
Love at first sight is also not for everyone. Usually it goes from seduction
(I'm curious about you), to conquering (I find you interesting), to surprising
(I like you more than I expected).
If you don't click right away with someone, remember that he might not be really
present. Perhaps he is in a difficult situation at work. Or maybe he has other
problems. Try to show understanding for the work predicaments others find
themselves in, if there is no spark between you. Everyone has difficulties
sometimes. It helps if we have more patience for each other.

*During a networking reception, I once stood next to a man with a sullen face.
He clearly made no effort to connect with others. I thought it was pitiful and when I
began a conversation with him, I soon realised why. He had nothing to say. He even
managed to answer open questions with some mumbling and he asked me nothing at
all. He appeared to have been sent by his boss to go networking. After a few difficult
moments I bid him a decent farewell, and told him honestly that I wanted to meet
some more people there.*

There are contacts you should grant your competitor

15. Negative statements

Gossip is the latest news about a person and is especially about negative things. Stories lead a life of their own because, consciously or unconsciously, things are invented. People usually draw the line with friends and family.

Gossip does not have to be negative, but it should not be hurtful. If it is not clear whether something is the truth then don't pass on a story or, even better, say that you don't know whether it is true. If you promised not to say anything then definitely don't! It is not only harmful to others but also for you. Your negative statements always come back to you through your network. People will get the impression that you might one day gossip about them. A gossip can, today or tomorrow, through social media, find themselves being talked about in undesirable places. Stay far away from this kind of thing and think about your reputation. An example of what gossip can do is featured in the film 'Gossip'.

Gossip is for some people like watching cnn.com: they become aware of what is happening. Of all Europeans the Dutch seem to gossip the most, according to a survey by Canon Europe in eighteen European countries among 5,500 office workers. Gossip is also a source of information and makes people feel connected. By jointly taking a position against another person, a bond is formed. I try to listen to rumours in corridors but don't participate. I don't directly believe what I hear, but do ask myself constantly in whose interest is it to spread a certain rumour.

Reputation comes on foot and leaves on horseback

50 Don'ts for Successful Business Networking

16. Ignore complaints

Don't ignore negative reactions but anticipate and try to solve any issues
in a sympathetic way. Research shows that an angry or offended customer
quickly shares their experience with up to twenty people in their network.
A satisfied customer on the other hand, shares his experience with up to twelve
people. Be good at your job and become a prominent specialist recommended by
word of mouth.
Nothing is more deadly for an organisation than to get negative publicity.
Especially through social media, a negative experience is rapidly distributed and
transmitted. For companies it is important to have a presence on social media at
least and listen carefully to what customers are saying online about the
company. It is therefore important for organisations to notice a negative
experience at an early stage and actually do something with it. Sign up for
Google Alerts and you will be notified by mail if your name is mentioned online.

*Some years ago I read the following true story. Guitar player Dave Carroll flew with
United Airlines. His guitar, which had a value of three thousand euros, was thrown
about when being handled and turned out to be severely damaged. Carroll got in touch
several times with United Airlines, but they ignored him. When eventually the cost was
not reimbursed, he decided to write a song about it with his band. The music was then
spread through social media and within two days it had been listened to 24,000 times.
By now the song has been viewed more than twelve million times on YouTube.
Only after Carroll promised to release two more songs, did United Airlines take action.*

Well done
is better than
well said

50 Don'ts for Successful Business Networking

17. Talk too much about yourself

In networking, it is important to listen. Let others talk as much as possible if they are interesting and you feel a connection. Don't talk too much about yourself. Make your elevator pitch no longer than a minute. Don't use jargon or distinguished language. Try telling a nice story that is in line with your listener's interests or makes your elevator pitch even more concrete and funny. Pay close attention to comments and approval.

Don't take yourself too seriously. Don't complain or talk in depth on a subject during an event or meeting. Create a personal follow-up appointment.

A discussion is also about giving and granting. One person says something and then it is the other's turn. You get attention and you give attention.

It should not be a presentation. Try to keep to these simple rules for an interesting conversation and do what you say you will.

A group of men at a networking event are talking with each other. Most talk about themselves and how great business is doing. They are not really listening. They are boasting, showing off and pretending it's all smooth sailing. One person has a remarkably different story and that's what I'd rather hear about. People don't want to hear fair weather stories. Also, imagine yourself vulnerable now and then. Tell a blooper. Share something that went difficult or even wrong. That makes you strong.

Nothing
influences
more than
recommendations

50 Don'ts for Successful Business Networking

18. Bragging

Don't brag about yourself and don't make things appear rosier than they are. Don't drop names and pretend you're great chums with well-known names but tell your story with passion so that others will remember you. Praising yourself is at the very least inappropriate and at worst a sin.

Self-promotion is a necessary component of getting the visibility you need to achieve your goals, but unfortunately, most people don't do it properly and come across as egos who exalt themselves. Self-promotion should be about giving and granting between you and the other. There are plenty of opportunities to promote yourself and they often come at unexpected moments. For example, when you are in a lift with a president or a director going to a reception, the financial manager at the coffee machine or the head of purchasing who also smokes outside. Always be prepared and have your elevator pitch ready.

Have you ever tried to do something that you are not so good at? I tried to play football in my youth. A boy next door always used to say to me that he was better than me. That boy was bragging. How do you feel when others do that? It is not very kind to show that you are better than someone else.

Let me speak a little more broadly. A few years ago, Samsung entered the Dutch market with its mobile phone. Siemens let them and looked haughtily down at them. They had an attitude of "we are the best." Siemens were indeed, in the beginning of the product life cycle. That was true for many of their products. The rest, as we say, is history...

no. 19
don'ts

The bigger
the ego,
the harder
the fall

50 Don'ts for Successful Business Networking

19. Career hunting

A good starting point to develop your management skills is your current job or task. Also do some internal networking without acting as a careerist or an over-achiever. Make sure you get additional responsibilities to supervise and manage people. A conversation with your manager or a conversation with the human resources department can help. This department often keeps notes on some possible next steps for different employees within a company. Your manager will recognise your leadership capabilities as they become visible. Provide evidence well in time, showing that you have ambition and are looking for concrete ways to expand your job's responsibilities.

Think mainly of increasing your responsibilities. If you want to prove that you are the right person, you make sure that in addition to your training, you showcase the required skills as well as your network contacts.

Henry was hired for a management position in a large electronics company. His manager was expecting to train him until he was ready for a position in management. Convinced that he was the man, Henry searched constantly for opportunities to display his talent. Unfortunately, he did not consider what his colleagues and managers thought of his behaviour. His manager had the impression that he was more concerned with climbing higher on the corporate ladder than with his current job. He soon gained a reputation as an overachiever. By the end, he had turned his internal network against him and alienated himself from the management team. It became unworkable for Henry and the last I heard was that he had left the company.

What's past
is past

20. Talk about the past

If you start a business at some later age, you tend to talk a lot about your employment history. Be aware of this habit, because it provides your frame of reference and your previous life. You are an entrepreneur and are considered to be thinking in a wider scope. We live in a different time now.
A time where everything changes fast. Gone are the days when we wrote letters by hand, or notes or articles were handed over to the secretaries in order to, depending on your status, wait and see how it looked typed up.
In those days, we would then wait for days to get a response; we also had to search in a library for relevant literature or buy books in a bookstore.
In short, the way we gather, process and provide, information happens quite differently than it did a dozen years or so ago. Don't talk unsolicited and inappropriately about the last century.

After I began my communications agency in the late nineties, I talked a lot about my time at Siemens. I talked about how we worked there. I also had a tendency, in the beginning, like in my former department, to brainstorm with clients about possible approaches. Customers sometimes watched me in confusion. It turned out that as small businesses, my clients were not always interested in the ways of such big international organisations. I made a deal with my clients that if I started talking about this without them asking, they would immediately correct me.

Give,
but don't
give away
your work

21. Give away

You can share knowledge and give away information, but if you are an adviser you must be careful not to give your advice away for free. You don't have to give everything away. Advising is your job, it is your bread and butter. Make a special appointment for it. What is a good thing indeed, is your unbiased and selfless commitment to a charity or a local initiative. But make it a conscious choice because you can only use your time once. A request to you is a form of giving back. The other person is, after all, giving you recognition for your expertise. Develop such habits in networking as thanking people or giving and receiving positive feedback. Despite the fact that many people think that gifts don't work, reality often shows just the opposite. However, it should be an gift that lingers over time and is connected to your product. It can be downright offensive when you give someone who doesn't drink, a bottle of alcohol. In the public sector, but also in large organisations, there are nowadays strict rules about the value of a gift.

Although my motto is "Give and Grant," I don't mean that you should give away work. When I started my business, I was sometimes invited to a business lunch by top managers. Typically, in a chic restaurant with three courses and a nice bottle of wine. I was honoured but soon the question would come: "How would you solve this or that?" I would then begin to hold forth on options. Back at home I would be left with the impression of a good conversation, but often I heard no more about it. Of course, what you have to do is make a timely follow-up appointment and then the meter for your consultation starts running.

Thou shall not stereotype

22. Prejudices

By dividing your market and determining your target group, you focus on certain people and not on others. Yet you must be careful to avoid prejudice. These days you cannot judge anyone by their appearance. A good networker is open to everyone, even to people who don't directly belong to their target group. You can learn a lot and get information that way. We live in a multicultural society and as an entrepreneur you have to open up, because not only do you have to live with it, but it is also a nice thing. A prejudice is an opinion that is not based on facts. Prejudices are dishonest, but that, unfortunately, is the world we live in.

It is impossible to process all the information about someone individually and therefore, groups are often linked by a single attribute. It is hard to rise above these prejudices. By knowing people or a group of people better, it is often clear that prejudices are based on false assumptions and are often not true.

Hetty is a financial adviser and long-standing member of an entrepreneurial club that I visit sometimes. Occasionally, a bowl is filled with members' business cards. Everyone draws a card and makes an appointment with that person. Hetty took Jasper's business card, a young web designer in jeans. She did not think it could be a valuable contact for her at all. However, during their conversation Jasper told her excitedly about his business. Hetty gave him six names he could call. She told her own story with the information that she specifically was looking for owners of family companies in the horticultural industry in the south of the Netherlands. A few weeks later Jasper sent her four addresses of people in her target group who were sent to him by one of his mother's uncles who supplied equipment to tomato growers. One of these growers has now become her client. Don't write people off on the basis of prejudice.

Put your cards
on the table

50 Don'ts for Successful Business Networking

23. Hidden agenda

A hidden agenda is an unspoken, personal objective which is generally contrary to the purpose of a call or a meeting. The opposite of a hidden agenda is an open agenda: the stated purpose that is communicated to everyone. This expression is derived from the technique of business meetings, where an agenda structures what items will be discussed.

In addition to meetings, hidden agendas are also applied in other forms of consultation, through negotiations and situations that are not directly related to the discussion. It can be said of a politician that he has a hidden agenda when his position in that case has one or more undisclosed intentions. The same happens deliberately in management teams of companies. Be aware of it.

The hidden agenda may be known by one or more parties. They are not open about their true intentions, perhaps because of matters of prestige or because a problem seems to be unsolvable. If one party does not suspect what the other really has in mind, the other may play their hidden agenda as their final trick. In both cases, the actual target is not on paper, nor even on the agenda. Often you will understand later why people reacted or behaved as they did. In the early days of my career I did not often immediately notice this, but later on I learned to live with it.

The world
becomes smaller,
your world
becomes bigger

50 Don'ts for Successful Business Networking

24. Social media as a goal

Companies have increasingly come to realise that they shouldn't use social media aimlessly. You need to pair it with your business goal: what do you want to achieve and how can social media deliver added value in achieving this objective? Think of it as a tool that can be very useful in combination with personal contacts. It is a pretty fast tool amongst communication tools. It is all about combining it with the 'traditional' methods of communication. In the end, you want to meet up to see what you can do for each other. Through social media you may well get in touch with your target group. Do this in steps: "What is your intended target group?" "Who are they and where are they located?" Find them online. The next step is to listen to your online network and understand their interests. Then make a plan with a strategy that you link to your goals. Only after you've done this you should get to work with, for example, a platform. Let your target group prove that you listened to them by tuning your message to their wishes and needs.

Social media should contribute to and ultimately play a role in improving business results. Yet I see companies that are unprofessional at handling social media. I believe it is therefore impossible that you leave the responsibility for this at the hands of a junior communications officer or, even worse, delegate it to a trainee. Junior staff may be absolutely indispensable because of their media knowledge and affinity but due to their lack of business experience and strategic knowledge they cannot be held responsible. The stakes are just too big. You want social media to create something positive with your target group, don't you?

If all things
are equal,
people prefer
to buy
from friends

25. Too many 'friends'

On social media especially, we tend to talk about friends. On LinkedIn, entrepreneurs have an average of 250 contacts. Some boast that they have more than 1000 contacts on LinkedIn or 2000 followers on Twitter. In reality, however, it is really about the quality of the contacts. On average we tend to only know five people well. By know well, means: you know their ambitions, you know their education, how many brothers and sisters they have and what hobbies they have. Let these precious relationships know what you can bring to them and what you want.

Unfriending has become a new verb and has even been elected as the word of the year. It is about cleaning up the online overgrowth in your friends list. Realise that college friends do not always stay friends. They become alumni, have careers or become successful entrepreneurs. Invest in these friends through regular contact. When they eventually occupy important positions, you will have a nice new entry.

Networking it is all about the quality of your contacts and not the quantity, I think. The personal network of friends of the average person consists of four to five people. Sociologist, Gerald Mollenhorst, came to establish this size on the basis of responses he received to the following questions: "Who do you discuss important personal matters with?", "Who would you ask for help for getting a job done in your house?" In seven years, half a private network seems to get replaced. In forty-six percent of cases, the reason for reduced or ended contact was a lack of meeting opportunities. Change in a relationship itself accounts for the fracture in only twelve per cent of cases.

He who cannot tweet will never be retweeted

26. Nonsense via social media

Social media is always a tool and not a goal in itself. Only a strategic approach, a vision and a policy will ultimately lead to the successful use of social media. It is ideal for intensifying new contacts, the sharing of knowledge, information gathering and maintaining contacts. It is very important that you determine what you want to communicate.

The big misconception about social media is that you participate because everyone does it, without knowing what message you want to spread. While there are a lot of opportunities, the great power of social media is that it creates engagement and interactivity. About eight per cent of messages on social media are spam. No less than forty percent of the new accounts on Twitter and Facebook are from spammers. Social media is a convenient and fun way to keep in touch with your target audience. Some people share everything with everybody and don't realise how the constant flow of information diarrhoea comes across. Use social media so you're not bothering people with non-information.

Facebook is perfect for uploading pictures of something you have just experienced. I don't upload everything I see or experience. Did you just take a balloon flight with some entrepreneurs and have a picture of the event? Upload it straight away! You recently had a new baby? It is nice to have time to share a cute picture of your child, but I don't like seeing things like that all the time! Or is your "baby" your beautiful new girlfriend? Perhaps your business isn't doing so well but does the rest of the world really need to know that? Use the time you might have spent nagging by instead doing something positive. Definitely share with your social networks when you have a new customer, if you have just got the key to your new office, or if your article has been published in a business magazine.

What's done
is done

50 Don'ts for Successful Business Networking

27. Misguided tweeting

Be conscious of what you put on social media. Is it relevant? Is it fun and informative? Does it do anything for the recipient? Do people like it? Or are you bothering them unsolicited like TV commercials disturbing a thrilling film or documentary. Read your text again and put yourself in your followers' shoes. Would you say it on a stage or in public? What do you want to achieve with it? It is on the internet and can go in any direction. Research shows that one in four people who had published something on social media like Twitter, saw afterwards that they shouldn't have done it.

The absence of 'normal' human interaction encourages people to say things on Twitter which they later regret. Tweeting on issues that you are not supposed to tweet about, for example: where you are and where you go. Do you think it is interesting that you have been invited to a party? With vague victory tweets such as, "Big order scored" we can do nothing ourselves but wonder how you are going to celebrate this with us. You are a specialist in a particular area so post a weekly tip about that. Give useful information,
do's and don'ts, tips and tricks.

I once read in the newspaper about the following sad accident: "A district police chief has been removed from her role because of a Twitter message. After a fatal accident in a house she posted on Twitter, 'Probably to do with domestic violence'." Later it turned out that the victims died through carbon monoxide poisoning. She had been previously warned and she understands the decision that was made and regrets it. So, be sure that you know what you're talking about when you're using Twitter.

Small gifts maintain the friendship

28. Only Christmas attention

Gifts obviously cost something and are inextricably linked to networking.
It must, however, involve a present that lingers in the mind, has a connection
with your product and is preferably not for sale everywhere. There are strict
rules for receiving gifts and this is especially true in government, but also in
large companies.
Invent a nice gift, something personal. Something useful for your relations,
something they react to positively, talk about and maybe even show to others in
their network. Traditionally there was the Christmas gift: a card, a calendar and
an diary. The calendar and diary are, as a gift, outdated. The best customers
usually receive a case of wine. Fortunately, it is becoming more common to raffle
these impersonal gifts amongst the staff. As a present provider you will need to
take this into consideration. Try to make contact on a number of other special
days. The advantage is that you will be more original and striking. Remember, it is
the little things and the details that matter.

More and more companies are opting for sending electronic Christmas or New Year cards,
saving paper and postage. They even communicate how much it saves. For example,
the company Ista published the following: they save about 900 kg of wood and more
than 16,000 litres of water. There are also companies whose cost-saving all go to charity.
So think about the message from the perspective of the relationship. A gift can be a tool
to convey that message or be a symbol for it. At the end of each year, I give the traditional
ChristmasTol (Christmas Stollen in Dutch which works as a play on my name, Tol), from
a local bakery with a nice personal letter or card. My clients' families already know this.
Over the course of the year, I unexpectedly give them something fun on Valentine's Day,
at Easter, summer holidays or on Saint Nicholas.

no. 29
don'ts

Look before
you leap

50 Don'ts for Successful Business Networking

29. Careless contact

Don't make personal information about or from your contacts available to others. Don't give out e-mail addresses and certainly not their mobile numbers. Maintain your integrity as regards to your contacts. Don't give out data for commercial purposes and definitely not without consulting your contacts first. Ask their permission.

If you have good and up-to-date information on your networking contacts then you often know more about your relations. Some of them have their strengths, but sometimes you also know their weaknesses. That does not mean that you can make those public. Within your network this rapidly becomes known, not appreciated, and makes it difficult to get new information in the future. Care is therefore required, otherwise your integrity is in danger. If you have a regular newsletter or publication that you send out, then make clear that if your subscribers want to remove themselves then you will delete their contact details. Don't spam. When people object that they are on a mailing list, remove them immediately from this list and tell them that it has been done.

I sometimes get asked about whether I know anyone who would like to do or sponsor something. And whether I would like to make an announcement about it and introduce them to the idea. I only do this if the questioner is someone with whom I have a friendly and trusting relationship, because it concerns my reputation. In a best-case scenario, I hand over the telephone numbers of potential contacts, but I also tell the contacts so that they know who will be getting in touch. If you synchronize contacts from your Outlook email, for example with your smartphone, make sure they are protected. In case of loss or theft of your smartphone other people's information is not out on the street. This also applies, of course, to your tablet and your laptop with this information.

Who
are you?
Who knows
you?

50 Don'ts for Successful Business Networking

30. Networking not necessary

Are you a civil servant? An employee? A lawyer? A specialist? A technician? Do you think you don't need to network? You have a good income and work comes naturally to you? Fantastic! But what if your contract does not get renewed? What if your sales pipeline dries up or your order book goes empty? Or your interim job stops because your customer goes bankrupt. Who can you contact?

You have never seriously built up your contacts, not comprehensively and you have certainly not maintained them. If you try to quickly resuscitate your contacts it will take a lot of your effort and time and in the short term you may not expect any results, especially if you are forcing it. Maybe, during the good times you should have invested more time in networking. But better late than never. Take a note of the do's in this book, practice them, and take my don'ts seriously. Attend a workshop, or even better, some training. It helps.

I read a response from Jayne on the internet about her perception of networking. She said she thinks of shows with lawyers on TV. Handsome, successful, young people, who know exactly the right way to start a conversation, walk tall, look right, make nice jokes and thoughtfully do exactly what they promise. "I am not like them and cannot be like them. I am scared when I talk to someone who remembers my holiday destination from last year. Help, am I being stalked? He is happy enough to talk to me, but five minutes later he has disappeared. How can you make acquaintances? Fortunately, as a freelance ICT-specialist I always have enough work from big clients. So I'm not urgently searching for new contacts." So far everything has been running smoothly for her ...

no. 31
don'ts

*Like
knows
like*

50 Don'ts for Successful Business Networking

31. Too long at one club

Some networks and business clubs tend to have an incestuous character. Everyone talks about the same things. There is a lot of talk about "us knowing us" and "that's the way we do things here." The result is that people end up in vicious cycles. It is important to provide variety for yourself.

So take part in more third-party networks to gain more and varied information. If you join a club, try to participate proactively and build bridges to other networks. Say goodbye, or get out if a networking club no longer meets your expectations or does not suit you anymore. There are business clubs where some members seem wedded to the furniture. They attend often and talk a lot, unfortunately usually about the same things. It is a cozy and solid club. There's nothing wrong with that, you might say. But young people don't feel really at home there and are often scared off by the regulars. Clubs are suffering due to the lack of new members and that's too bad because young people often provide new impulses and that is refreshing.

I am never a member of a single business club for too long because I also need to meet others. I have seen it happen often after all these years. I will always be a loyal and an active member. I am also a member of a club outside of my operational field. Recently I did quit one such a club where knowledge sharing was very important. For example, the evenings spent at the lecture hall of Erasmus University had always been very interesting as they were about current affairs. But then the person in charge and two active members in the club were forced to leave because of their busy work as entrepreneurs. It all faded rapidly after that. Part of the old guard kept coming but the youngsters did not.

Don't search
high and low

50 Don'ts for Successful Business Networking

32. Overstay at events

Often the same people join in at events, as if they have nothing better to do. They ensure that they will be invited anywhere or they even arrive unannounced. They don't want to miss anything and will attend more than one New Year's drinks party on the same evening in January. They want to be seen and known and often make a beeline straight for the 'important' people. They often keep hanging around, don't leave at the peak of the evening and ignore signals and even announcements that the event has ended. Don't do this. Instead, focus on an interesting event where you have previously asked who is on the participants list. Also skip an event when it has become predictable: it's the same people in the same environment. Professional networking is a mix between personal contact and result-oriented work. Unfortunately, almost no one naturally has both skills. Only if you are conscious of it you can work on it. If you want to network in a result-oriented way, then you have to set goals – even for each event. Be proactive, set the tone, and define the topic of conversation.

Exceptions prove the rule as shown by the following example. I am talking about the 'Jan des Bouvrie' effect. He was a designer on the television show 'Glamourland'. The show invariably showed Jan saying, "Hello! Here we are again!" Jan was present at as many events as were going on where photography and television recordings were made. He had not the slightest objection to this. He said more than once during interviews that his appearances in 'Glamourland' increased his personal branding and hence his order backlog. However, as a society figure, he was regularly the subject of ridicule.

If you drink,
you become
another being...
with more thirst

50 Don'ts for Successful Business Networking

33. Just for fun

If you go to a networking event, try to be sober and stay that way, even if it is only out of respect of the organiser and those taking part. Don't drink beforehand. It is a myth that you will be more sociable and more daring if you drink. In the best scenario, you will be somewhat more talkative, but you'll find yourself saying things you'll later regret. Drinks are often in abundance at such events, so in between drinks, have a drink without alcohol. Ultimately, you are not at the pub. Also remember that the events are often photographed. You don't want to be published in a business magazine, or worse, permanently on the internet, known as a party animal, do you? The event is organised for a purpose and has a finishing time. Leave at the high point, after having thanked the organiser, of course.

Nowadays you can't smoke inside so do so in the designated area, where you can network with fellow smokers. Don't throw your cigarette away, but put it in the ashtray and put a mint in your mouth on your return. You don't want the people to who you are talking to be confronted with your smoky breath, do you?

A good, free business networking event that I always attend takes place every first Tuesday of the month. It takes place in the bar of the local theatre at the end of the day. It has been organised successfully for many years by the local association of entrepreneurs and the municipality. Sixty entrepreneurs attend. The mayor and councillors are regularly attendants, so you can easily talk with them. It needs to finish by 19:00 and everything must be cleared up so that staff can prepare for the evening show. However, there are always visitors still drinking and trying to stay longer. This is not what the meeting is intended for. That's what the pub next door is for...

Don't harry someone

50 Don'ts for Successful Business Networking

34. Stalking and sticking around

There are people who want to talk to decision makers so badly that they literally chase them and, like asps, keep buzzing around them. There is no way for these decision makers to ignore them. These quasi 'networkers' are all over you and often become stickers. They start a substantive conversation where you can't get involved, but time progresses and you want to meet more people or even want to leave. They often start complaining and whining. How can you get rid of them? You could end a conversation with them in the following way: "Sorry, I want to speak to a few other people, I wish you luck."

When you bombard people with business offers and continually tell them why you are so good, they will be inclined to not choose you. You are then stalking rather than networking. This applies both online and offline. This is one reason, that I know from personal experience, why decision makers don't often attend certain meetings or participate in platforms on the internet.

Both online and offline stalking have one common characteristic: irritation. With online stalking, there is no physical contact involved. This allows the preconception that this is worse than offline stalking. The threshold for cyberstalking is lower than physical stalking because the stalker has no personal contact with the victim. For the cyber stalker the danger seems to be smaller. They can remain anonymous and bother anyone they want to from behind a nickname. When online I make sure I have a good spam filter. Offline I have developed a few strategies which I have written about in this book.

Actions
speak louder
than words

50 Don'ts for Successful Business Networking

35. Yourself in foreground

It is not important that everyone sees you. What counts is that the right people see you and that their image of you is positive. Don't put yourself at the forefront with overactive exposure in public. The other extreme is to keep yourself in the background. You should not want to stand out as a networker too obviously or behave within your network as a cocky know-it-all.

The world has a number of successful business people who are constantly in the spotlight. Conversely, there are entrepreneurs who work more in the background. It is not necessary to be a world-famous citizen. It is much more interesting to be a famous person in the target group that is relevant to you. Your image then works as a nice reference. Your business will be more pleasant, especially if you notice that information, entertainment, or even orders come to you straight away. In the spotlight or outside the spotlight? You yourself? Or your brand? Do it sparingly.

I have heard a lot about Aad Ouborg but never of Amancio Ortega. Aad is a Dutch entrepreneur and inventor, and was the founder of the household brand Princess. He has received many awards. Aad has invented a special way of marketing and that is, to have fun together with his network of customers – 'Business is Entertainment'. After the sale of Princess, this multimillionaire presented the TV show 'Topmanager wanted'. But who knows Amancio Ortega? He is the founder of the clothing company Inditex. Every week he is at the opening of establishments around the world and has more than 14,000 employees. This Spaniard is a billionaire but unknown and is rarely publicised, unlike his retail chain Zara.

You can't
judge a book
by its cover

50 Don'ts for Successful Business Networking

36. Forget controllers

The role of the controller within organisations has, especially in bad economic times, more and more importance. Research by the Financial Times shows that more than half of the CFOs (Chief Financial Officers) find that their status has been growing in recent years. No longer are they seen internally as dull and boring accountants. Rather, the CFO of today is a strategic partner who facilitates doing business. He is trained and responsible for the management information flow. As a result he is forced to become more approachable and to develop his social skills.

Since the economic crisis, the CFO must boost confidence in the financial health of the organisation. He will occasionally have to show up at network events. So he needs to network and you should network with him. Wander along with him and ask how business goes. Or ask what clients are in the top ten of his company this year. He can tell you exactly. What interests him? What hobbies does he have? Try to 'click' with him.

During an entrepreneurs' lunch I sat next to a networking contact. The conversation came around to a good new customer that he had. It was a company whose general manager was sitting at another table at the same event. I also knew him as financially responsible, because we were both members at Club 25. When I asked my neighbour at the table if he knew Eric, he answered in the negative. "Shall I introduce him to you?" I asked. He wanted that very much. After coffee, I went over to Eric and I asked him if I could introduce him to the general manager of one of his suppliers. He said the historic words, "That's the company whose invoices I regularly sign." He had no idea who was behind this company. I introduced the two men to each other and let Eric sit in my seat. Eric could now put a face to the company.

The more
people you know,
the more
you know

50 Don'ts for Successful Business Networking

37. Talking to strangers

You go to a networking event and meet someone with whom you have a conversation. It is someone who seems to listen well. You are not used to it. You start to tell them more and more, all about your job and information about your work. You do this without knowing exactly where he works and why he is actually there. He listens to you in a sympathetic manner. When you ask for his card half an hour later, you find out that he appears to be a competitor who you really didn't want to divulge so much information to. Always ask in a timely fashion the open question, "What brings you here?" Or, if it is too late, "What is the reason you're asking me this?"

A substantive, in-depth talk with someone is certainly not the intention of an event such as this. Make a separate appointment in a quiet area where you cannot be disturbed. You attend an event specifically to meet other people.

A few years ago I went to an ICT-event in the middle of Amsterdam. There were also informal investors there. I fell into conversation with a domineering guy who was especially interested in sales, growth and money. He was interrogating me and I dutifully replied. Afterwards I didn't have a good feeling about it. But just before I decided to leave I found out that you could also meet nice people there. Jan came from the same region as me and told me he had just founded an online company. We clicked immediately and he has become a dear business friend of mine. I nominated him to be director of a Chamber of Commerce initiative. I have worked for this initiative and for his company.

We're in this together

38. Always together

Pay attention to the person you've asked to accompany you to an event.
If your partner does not like 'the networking obligation' it soon becomes evident.
You will be inhibited by this and you'll end up paying too much attention to
your partner to make sure they're having a good time. In short, you are going to
behave atypically. Go alone or go along to the type of event where you will both
get some fun out of it. Or go with someone who also brings his partner with him.
The partners at least can have a chat with each other. You could get to the event
together or even eat something together beforehand. If you arrange to go to an
event with a colleague or a friend, then the chances are you'll stick together as a
duo and you won't have enough 'space' to network with others. So, agree in
advance that you won't stay stuck together and tell them why you need to do
this. Don't let them stand on their own but instead introduce them to
acquaintances early on. Naturally then, the saying should go: "Arrive together
and leave together."

*My partner does not always find going to a meeting enjoyable. She won't know many
people and is often introduced to one after another. For you it is familiar territory
with familiar faces. My partner doesn't always come along and I understand that.
She deliberately chooses meetings where there will be acquaintances of hers and
some more women. She opts for events with added value such as a concert, a theatre
performance or a golf day where our roles are often reversed.*

Fine feathers
make fine birds

39. Underdressed and overdressed

You only have a very little time to make a good first impression so make sure that what you wear is appropriate. Better to be somewhat overdressed than underdressed for a business meeting or invitation. Below are the official dress codes, so you at least know what to wear.

'Tenue de ville': as long as your clothes are neat, you can wear whatever you like. Often it is in combination with a jacket, nowadays often without a tie.

At many meetings, it is appropriate to dress 'Business casual'. For women this consists of neat trousers or skirt with a shirt or sweater. 'Business Casual Classic' is the most business-like style. A jacket with dress pants, shirt and possibly a tie or a pocket square. Or a suit with a sporty look. 'Business Casual Smart' is more free: neat jeans and a sweater or shirt with a jacket. 'Business Casual Relaxed' is still neat, but sporting a sweater or cardigan. 'Black Tie' means a tuxedo with a white tuxedo shirt with double cuffs and a blind closure. You wear shiny leather, black shoes and black socks. There is no belt so there will be suspenders. Women wear a short or long evening dress with modest neckline and gloves.

It is useful to know what to wear to a specific meeting to make u good impression. Check what the invitation recommends about what to wear. I pay a lot of attention to my clothing. Our councillor dresses in jeans when he speaks with local residents, but normally he wears suits, because he feels good dressed like that. The politician Pim Fortuyn also spoke regularly with local residents, but completely dressed in suit and silk tie. Why? Because it emphasised his authenticity. People would pay attention to him anyway though.

Hear no evil,
see no evil
and speak
no evil

40. Breaking into group discussions

When people stand very close to each other in a group, they are intimate and you shouldn't break in. If there is clearly more space between them, then look to make eye contact with one of the speakers. If successful, the group will split apart. This is a natural kind of behaviour. Say hello and don't start talking, but take another moment. Often we don't because we are too tense.

According to research, each person tries to maintain four zones. The intimate zone is a circle of half a metre, and is used in, for example, a confidential conversation. In a personal zone, the circle can be more than a metre, such as at a conference. The social zone is a circle of almost four metres such as seen, for example, at a reception; and a public zone is more than about four metres and can be seen, for example, at an exhibition. Introverted people have a lot of trouble breaking in during a conversation. Extroverted people have clearly smaller circles than introverted people and find it easier to enter these circles than others do.

You probably know the type of situation: at an event or in the corridors of a company, a group of people are talking or arguing. You see an acquaintance among them and would like to join the group. But how do you mix in this group? If it is a closed wall, it is very difficult. I always make eye contact and see if I am welcome. If not, I walk on or wait for my turn. The best part is that you get involved in a natural way and are introduced to everyone if they are unknown to you. The best that can happen is that a participant explains briefly what they are talking about and you can join in with the conversation.

I don't have
an office,
I am an office

41. Taking calls during conversations

Since the creation of the smartphone, its use has changed dramatically when you are in company and with other people. However, there are more and more sessions where it is expected that you will send a text message during a presentation or workshop. At those times you can leave it on but keep the sound off! In small groups put the phone on vibrate mode and say upfront that you may be called for an urgent matter. You have then explained the necessity of using it.

It is undoubtedly rude to sit in company and text or message with WhatsApp. Young people and students do this a lot because they are more used to it. Adults who are bored when sitting in meetings also do this, or they check their mail. It can be very irritating and it is up to the chairman whether he involves these people in the meeting. If you are having a serious one-on-one meeting with someone or you are in a small group, then you should not be keeping in touch with other people at the same time. Not by tablet, phone, mobile, text messages, WhatsApp and certainly not via Skype.

People under thirty-five years old are more casual about the way they use a mobile to communicate than I am. However, we shouldn't underestimate the number of people in my age group who talk at top volume and blare into their mobile phones while on public transport or in restaurants. In social situations, the rule has always been that you just don't do that. You don't interrupt ongoing conversations to start exchanging gossip with a third person. For young people like my son it is different it seems. They have never had a landline. They always have their smartphone with them, and it is always on. Where their identity is involved it is an extension of themselves.

*Asking
questions
makes you
wiser*

50 Don'ts for Successful Business Networking

42. Asking closed questions

If you want to know more about a person and his problems, you will have to listen more than you talk. It is about asking the right and sensible questions. Questions can be split into categories. They can be divided into open, closed and leading questions.

Closed questions are questions where someone has to answer with a "yes" or a "no" and you will not learn much by using them. Make clear what you want from a listener, for example, by starting with a closed question: "Do you have fifteen minutes to listen and then give me your opinion? I'll try to set something straight" or "Do you have half an hour to listen to me?" Hopefully the answer to these closed questions is a positive "Yes". Then move on to using open questions. Listen carefully: you will be amazed how many people will tell you interesting things if you keep silent and listen. Targeted open questions ensure that you get to know the other person better and you get used to each other. The focus then will smoothly move to you. Encourage others to talk by nodding or humming. Or ask, "How interesting. How do you do that?" Or "Tell me more about that, please."

It is important to ask the right type of question in a networking conversation that takes place after your elevator pitch. Ask many open questions. Do this especially at an initial meeting; for example, at an event and if you want to learn something. For example: "Good morning, what brings you here?" "Good afternoon, I was invited by..." "How do you know...?" "What kind of business are you in?" "What trends do you see for your industry?" I practice the echo technique. For example:

He: We build sustainable offices.

Me: I've read a lot about this lately!

He: Yes, it's an opportunity for us in the market at the moment.

Me: May I ask what you do to make the most of this opportunity?

After this open question it is time to listen, listen, listen...

Don't look over someone's shoulder

50 Don'ts for Successful Business Networking

43. Looking away

Always focus on the person you are talking to. Don't keep looking past them all the time to see whether there are other, perhaps more important, people around. This makes the other person feel as if they are not an interesting conversationalist. It is not good for one's self-confidence. It is sometimes difficult not to do it, because there are often people walking around who are normally difficult to tackle. There may be managers, for example, who are normally, if you call them, shielded by assertive secretaries.

If you see in the corner of your eye someone who you absolutely must speak to, and he or she wants to leave, then be honest with your current partner and tell them. Excuse yourself and walk over to the person who you want to speak to and ask if he has some time later on. Then go back to your partner and pick up the thread of the discussion again. Do this only if your discussion is just about exchanging information and not if you are in the middle of a story or somewhere in your own story. Try to finish this first.

Perhaps you've met someone in the past who introduces himself to you, then quickly asks about what you do, nods and increasingly spends his time looking over your shoulder and ends up turning his back to you. This person suspects that he probably can't earn anything from you. How did you feel when that happened? Don't do it, therefore, to another. If there is no connection, then I can imagine that it does not make much sense to stay in a conversation. At those times I end the conversation in a respectful manner. I say I want to meet more people and provide a decent farewell. He may have already given me his business card but in these circumstances I don't give mine. He probably won't ask for it anyway!

My name
is
nobody

44. Forget names

Calling people by the right name is an important business skill. People like it when their name is remembered and do business faster with you if you call them by name. For most people, associating names with faces remains a hell of a job. That is unfortunate because remembering names impresses others. Remember that a person's name is the most wonderful sound to them. Focus on what they are saying and take a few seconds to let yourself absorb the name. Repeat the name after the introduction. Do that once or twice, very subtly: "Nice meeting you, Ray." Does the person you've just been introduced to have an uncommon name? Then it helps to talk about it. "Gosh, I don't come across that name very often. Where does that name come from?" Associate the name with something! "Have you just been introduced to Bill?" Then get Bill Gates on your mind. Or connect the name you have just heard to a friend, relative or neighbour with the exact same name.

Many people who meet or speak to each other forget each other's names. That is human. I solve it in the following way: "I know you from somewhere. I cannot quite remember, though. Can you tell me your name again, please?" Then give some thought to the name of the other person and make associations with it. Armed with a smartphone, you can exchange virtual cards with new contacts. This is also a good way to imprint names. I discovered the app Evernote Hello. With this you don't just write down a name and remember the place of encounter, but also attach a picture. Pictures especially make it easier to remember. For that reason, I put my face, the same picture as on my LinkedIn profile, on my business card.

no. 45
don'ts

It's not
what you say,
it's what
people hear

45. Treasure age

Don't be tempted to guess someone's age. Even if they ask you to explicitly and emphatically. These people especially want to hear you say a younger age. If you are pressed then say you are no good at it. If you absolutely cannot avoid it then estimate that they are quite a few years younger.

This is particularly sensitive for women. Nowadays it is more difficult to estimate because we look much younger. Hair is coloured, faces lifted, clothing and the way we speak have been rejuvenated.

It remains difficult to estimate a person's age. You can see it on the hands, but that's only with people who are a bit older. With younger people it is even more difficult. More than eighty percent of women think they look younger than their peers. So watch out with estimating. You can practise better estimating a person's age by their appearance on the website howoldareyou.net.

After a conference and at a networking reception once, I was talking with a woman who worked in real estate. We talked about business and at one point we talked about how many years we had been entrepreneurs. I told her that I had been working for more than twenty-five years in business before I started my own business. When she asked how old I was. I replied, whereupon she immediately asked: "How old do you think I am?" I guessed her as four years older than she was. The conversation ground to a halt even though I tried to soften it up with some compliments. But it became increasingly painful... I had messed up hopelessly, I realised. There was a long silence and she broke it by saying that she had to visit the ladies' room and left with a "See you later" ...

Knowing you
is
loving you

50 Don'ts for Successful Business Networking

46. Awe for VIPs

Don't have exaggerated respect for celebrities, but instead have respect for them. Once they were unknown and they had unattainable ideals and heroes. Often they find it nice if you say "Hi" and don't have any further intentions than to thank them or to ask them to be photographed with you.

Titles should also not scare you off. Sometimes these are people who have learned a lot in specific areas. Nothing human is strange to them. Don't hesitate to start a conversation with them about nothing at all! Often it is in another area where you may connect over something and you may find things in common with your business. Ask for a business card, and if you get the chance to say something about yourself, then make sure you ask if you can email them some time. But take care: they are often asked to commit themselves without compensation. They can, if you approach them honestly and sincerely, open doors that would normally remain closed to you.

If you have a hero, then sometimes respect and appreciation can turn into awe and this can block the communication. Sometimes this is not nice for the recipient. In my case, this happened with Ray Davies, the lead singer of The Kinks, for whom I have had huge admiration since my youth. He is an idiosyncratic musician and storyteller. I have seen his band perform a few times live in the sixties and seventies, and I saw Ray himself perform several times in the Netherlands. So I am a big fan. I recently shook hands with him on stage at the Theatre Carré Amsterdam and put him on a pedestal. I realise it now. I didn't even know what to say to him. Or, actually I did, with a question about his statement: "My name is of no importance; I am a faceless man. One day I will become an individual."

Support the one
you see
in the mirror

50 Don'ts for Successful Business Networking

47. Name dropping

In a conversation, mentioning the names of famous people you apparently know, in order to show that you're also important, is called name dropping. Now and then, when it suits and it fits in with the context, you can mention the name of a well-known person you really do know. But don't go scattering it around like, "I know a lot of important people." Who do you know really well? We don't even know our neighbours. And especially not the hundreds of contacts we have online. Be honest: who has time for more than a handful of real friends? Most people have about five friends, no more! It's unlikely that there is a celebrity amongst them. So be critical of people who name-drop and don't start doing it yourself, unless there really is a famous person in your inner circle, of course.

Name dropping is bragging with famous people's names. On the other hand, if you really know someone well, you can, of course mention it. If it fits into the context and you can bring people together and help someone with information or even an introduction to your contact. Often they have protected addresses and phone numbers. Obviously, you should not give out sensitive information, but you can introduce someone or propose something to a famous entertainer or a specialist. If you know him well, that is...

Hollow
phrases
sound the
loudest

50 Don'ts for Successful Business Networking

48. Buzzwords

Avoid buzzwords such as "we'll keep in touch" when saying goodbye. Make a specific appointment at the end of a business conversation. Put the appointment directly in your agenda, your smartphone or on the back of the business card you have received. Respond within two days, even if it is not a firm arrangement yet or if it is difficult to fit around your current schedule. Add a bit of information, no matter how brief, into your CRM/Outlook.

People often say out of habit, "We should meet up some time," or "Let's have a cup of coffee or a quick business lunch sometime." If you say you want to meet, immediately pull out your calendar or smartphone for an appointment. If you don't really want a follow-up then don't say it. It's the same when making an appointment without obligations, one that is too vague or unclear. If you make an appointment, don't cancel it at the last moment, for example because you still need to finish your quotation. You then get on the slippery slope of sliding arrangements.

My experience with people who finish a conversation with "We should make an appointment," is that it's vague. I usually try to schedule a follow-up appointment by pulling out my smartphone but these people still sometimes do the difficult thing and respond with "I'll call you," or "I'll mail you." In the best case scenario, they may say, "Can you email me a proposed date?" You then often don't get a direct response. My advice is to let your instincts play a major role and don't insist on a follow-up. If they want to keep in contact, then by all means do so, but not with a "noncommittal or vague" appointment.

no. 49

don'ts

No second
chance
for a good
first
impression

50 Don'ts for Successful Business Networking

49. Strewing business cards around

You know the type of people who set out with piles of business cards in order to score the same amount back. They go for many contacts instead of friendly and more personal ones. Everyone they encounter must have their card and they want one back as quickly as possible. They hop like bees in a flower bed at a networking event. The next morning they barely know who was who. On most cards, unfortunately, there is no picture, so after two days they don't even know who they were talking to. You often receive a newsletter that shows that you are on their mailing list.

Make sure you always have business cards on hand and not in your hand. Asking if you can give someone your business card is a lot friendlier than pushing it under someone's nose. The real networkers also ask for an additional card for when they see opportunities with someone else from their networking contacts. Pay a compliment to the design of the card. Perhaps the logo or the name makes you think of something you can mention. Process the data within two days in your database or Outlook.

Thinking of sprinkling out business cards and laying them out on a table so that everyone can pick one up? Don't! What I always do is the following: ask for someone's card as soon as possible, study it and hope that the other person will ask for my card. If not, then I ask them if I can give my card. Beware of the recipient's response. Will it be accepted and tucked away immediately? This may be an indication of little interest. Will it be gladly received, viewed and even asked about? If they do, in my experience, the newly acquired contact deserves it to be followed up in any case.

Your face
speaks
volumes

50 Don'ts for Successful Business Networking

50. Storing business cards

A businessman receives an average of over fifty business cards a year. They often disappear in stacks gathered together by an elastic band, to be entered at some point in a data file, or in beautiful folders. Nowadays, with an app such as ScanBizCards for iPhone, a business card can be easily digitized and incorporated into Outlook. Around Christmas or an event, the file is usually a priority again when the salespeople and account managers are busy with the mailing list. Don't let business cards you've received just lie around on your desk but store them neatly and put them in your database.

Also, don't put cards you've received in your shirt's breast pocket. There is nothing wrong with that you might say, but you have to remember to then get them out when you put your shirt in the washing machine. When ironing you'll find some white flakes whirling around on the ironing-board. If you had forged some close relationships with the intent to enter them in your Outlook and you had a follow up in mind, you will now have to dig them out of your memory. Hopefully you'll get a LinkedIn request...

Desperately, I looked at the wallets full of cards, while almost everyone is now active on the internet, especially on LinkedIn. Maybe I should decide to just "not have one" to stand out from everyone else. As a networking professional I feed all the business cards I receive into Outlook as soon as possible and naturally I have a smartphone with me where I can find my contacts. Where I can, I connect with others via the LinkedIn app and where that fails, I ask for a card. Right then I make sure I have set up a moment of connection and in the long term they will receive status updates. Even so, a few weeks ago I ordered yet again a couple of boxes of business cards with my picture on them.

The don'ts are often things you have learned yourself and they are sometimes not good for your network. Try working on them in conjunction with the do's you are doing or planning to do.

Be aware what you definitely should not do:

1.	See networking as goal	*6.*	Forced networking
2.	Passive networking	*7.*	Networking when you have to
3.	See networking as a trick	*8.*	Confuse selling with networking
4.	Expect others to help you	*9.*	Keeping quiet
5.	Pretend you're interested	*10.*	Neglecting your family

50 questions to assess yourself

How efficiently do you network?
Take the test!

1 = never 2 = occasionally 3 = frequently 4 = often 5 = always   Score

Knowing your strengths as a networker
1. I know what the important values and principles are in my life. ____
2. I can recall at least five successes in my (business) life. ____
3. I am clear about my knowledge, skills and the help I can offer. ____
4. I use social media purposefully. ____
5. I know my own strengths as a networker. ____
6. I have a networking plan. ____

____ +

Being clear and friendly in networking
7. I professionally present myself, what I do, and what I can do for others. ____
8. I introduce myself clearly, concisely and arouse interest. ____
9. I feel comfortable in groups and start conversations effectively. ____
10. I focus my full attention on new people so they remember me. ____
11. I find it easy to act as host/hostess at networking events. ____
12. I create visibility for myself and my organisation. ____
13. I am friendly and considerate to everyone I meet. ____

____ +

Using business cards effectively
14. My card is a good representation of who I am and what I do. ____
15. I always have my business cards at hand. ____
16. I give my business card when appropriate. ____
17. I make notes on cards I receive as reminders to myself. ____

____ +

Cherishing and nurturing your network by appreciation

18. I express appreciation regularly both offline and online. _____
19. I maintain my network in appropriate ways with various tools. _____
20. I send cards, emails, links, tweets and apps with a personal note. _____
21. I receive and regularly provide gratitude and support. _____

_____ +

Networking efficiently

22. I have for my network an effective system for organisation and search. _____
23. My business card records are in order and updated in my database. _____
24. I'd rather get things done than add more items to my to do list. _____
25. I call or mail someone back within 24 hours. _____
26. I organise my thoughts before I contact a person. _____
27. I say no to activities that would be at the expense of my time or energy. _____
28. I prepare networking events to optimally exploit the opportunity. _____
29. I evaluate and adjust my network on a regular basis. _____

_____ +

Being effective with your questions and contacts

30. I ask and use the help of others. _____
31. I make requests of my network in a clear manner. _____
32. I always find an opportunity to ask: "Do you know someone who ...?" _____
33. I take immediate action on leads. _____
34. I find any contact valuable. _____

_____ +

Staying in the picture by participation and cooperation

35. I am a member of entrepreneurial or professional associations. _____
36. I have a role at a club, or on the board of an organisation. _____
37. I often refer to my network. _____
38. I always try to go the extra mile for my clients. _____

_____ +

Developing a personal networking approach

39. I trust and follow my intuition.

40. I feel obliged to contribute something to the success of my network.

41. I am known for my service.

42. I am an active and attentive listener.

43. I am open to every opportunity in my network.

44. I regularly organise my own networking event.

＿＿＿ +

Networking to give your (business) life more substance

45. I am known as an influential networker with a large network.

46. I use networking for myself and others.

47. My network is usually at the forefront of my mind.

48. I am an example for influential long-term networking.

49. I see the world as one big network. Both offline and online.

50. Networking is fun and a way of life for me.

＿＿＿ +

Total: ＿＿＿

Your score is on www.networkacademy.nl

This test was created on the basis of a design by Slooter and Partners from the network book of Gerard D. de Gier

www.ingramcontent.com/pod-product-compliance
Lightning Source LLC
Chambersburg PA
CBHW070522200326
41519CB00013B/2894

LES
CODES FRANÇAIS

COLLATIONNÉS

SUR LES ÉDITIONS OFFICIELLES

contenant :

1° LA CONFÉRENCE DES ARTICLES ENTRE EUX ;

2° SOUS CHAQUE ARTICLE LES TEXTES TANT ANCIENS QUE NOUVEAUX QUI LES
EXPLIQUENT, LES COMPLÈTENT OU LES MODIFIENT ;

3° UN SUPPLÉMENT PAR ORDRE ALPHABÉTIQUE ET CHRONOLOGIQUE,
RENFERMANT, OUTRE LES LOIS LES PLUS USUELLES, CELLES
EXIGÉES POUR LES THÈSES ET LES TEXTES ANCIENS
QUI SONT ENCORE EN VIGUEUR ;

4° UNE TABLE ALPHABÉTIQUE RENVOYANT AUX LOIS ET AUX
PAGES OU ELLES SONT REPRODUITES,

ET

Les seuls où sont rapportés

LES TEXTES DU DROIT ANCIEN ET INTERMÉDIAIRE

NÉCESSAIRES A L'INTELLIGENCE DES ARTICLES

PAR

LOUIS TRIPIER

Avocat à la Cour d'appel de Paris, Docteur en droit, ex-Membre du Conseil
général de l'Yonne.

CODE NAPOLÉON ET CONSTITUTION.

PARIS

LIBRAIRIE DE JURISPRUDENCE DE COTILLON

RUE DES GRÉS-SORBONNE, 16.

1853